2014 CODING WORKBOOK

for the Physician's Office

2014 CODING WORKBOOK for the Physician's Office

Alice Covell, CMA-A (AAMA), RMA, CPC

Australia • Brazil • Mexico • Singapore • United Kingdom • United States

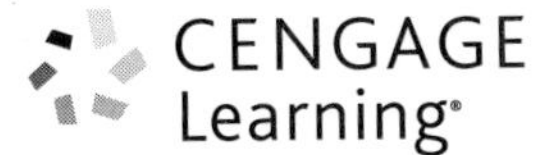

2014 Coding Workbook for the Physician's Office
Alice Covell

VP, General Manager, Skills and Planning: Down Gerrain

Product Director: Stephen Helba

Senior Director, Development-Careers and Computing: Marah Bellegarde

Product Manager: Jadin Babin-Kavanaugh

Senior Content Developer: Elisabeth Williams

Editorial Assistant: Nicole Manikas

Marketing Director: Michele McTighe

Marketing Manager: Erica Glisson

Production Manager: Andrew Crouth

Content Project Management, and Art Direction: PreMediaGlobal

The 2014 versions of CPT, ICD-9-CM, ICD-10-CM, and ICD-10-PCS were used in preparation of this product.

Library of Congress Control Number: 2014934995

Book Only ISBN: 978-1-285-44163-4
Package ISBN: 978-1-285-44139-9

Cengage Learning
5 Maxwell Drive
Clifton Park, NY 12065-2919
USA

Cengage Learning is a leading provider of customized learning solutions with office locations around the globe, including Singapore, the United Kingdom, Australia, Mexico, Brazil, and Japan. Locate your local office at **www.cengage.com/global.**

Cengage Learning products are represented in Canada by Nelson Education, Ltd.

To learn more about Cengage Learning, visit **www.cengage.com**

Purchase any of our products at your local college store or at our preferred online store **www.cengagebrain.com.**

Printed in the United States of America
1 2 3 4 5 6 7 18 17 16 15 14

Contents

Preface

Organization of the Text

The *2014 Coding Workbook for the Physician's Office* is organized in the easiest to understand and most logical format currently available in the market for students and instructors alike. The workbook begins with the basics, a brief foundational overview of the importance of coding and the tools necessary to succeed using this text. It is designed to be used in tandem with any main textbook or as supplemental study material.

The workbook begins with coding scenarios for Current Procedural Terminology (CPT), utilizing Evaluation and Management (E/M) codes and is broken down by body system and then by service performed. The CPT scenarios are followed by HCPCS Level II and CPT and HCPCS Modifiers coding exercises. The bulk of the workbook is comprised of ICD-10-CM and ICD-9-CM coding scenarios. The workbook concludes with case studies, "Putting It All Together," where students can review a case study and provide proper codes based on the practice they've had using the workbook. Answers to the case studies are provided in the back of the workbook.

In the final preparation for students, the workbook offers exam questions for CPT, CPT and HCPCS, and ICD-10-CM. Selected answers from coding exercises are also provided in the back of the book to enhance student comprehension.

New to *2014 Coding Workbook for the Physician's Office*

As 2015 approaches, so too does the shift to using ICD-10-CM in medical coding. In anticipation of this industry change, the *2014 Coding Workbook for the Physician's Office* includes an updated section entitled "Moving from the old ICD-9-CM to the new ICD-10-CM." This section provides students with an overview of the major changes that medical coding will be facing and challenges students to start coding with ICD-10-CM. Also, "Putting It All Together" includes a column for ICD-10-CM codes in the answers.

In addition to the chapter on ICD-10-CM, a secondary answer column has been provided next to the ICD-10-CM answers for ICD-9-CM. All of the coding scenarios have been updated to be applicable with ICD-10-CM coding guidelines. Students will not only have the benefit of learning to code with the ICD-10-CM system but also supplement their practice and enhance their knowledge with ICD-9-CM codes that may still be used by Worker's Compensation and the auto insurance industry. This significant contribution to the *2014 Coding Workbook for the Physician's Office* embraces the future of coding in the same easy-to-understand and logical format that has been a success since its first publication!

Supplement Package

For the Student

- A 59-day free trial of OptumInsight©'s *EncoderPro.com—Expert* is provided as a bind-in card in the front of the workbook. This software will allow students to look up ICD-9-CM, ICD-10-CM, CPT, and HCPCS Level II codes quickly and accurately across all code sets.
- AAPC continuing education unit (CEU) approval is granted after candidates successfully pass the 30-question exam posted on Cengage Learning's Premium Web site. For more information please see the back page of the workbook.

For the Instructor

- The *Instructor's Manual* is housed online at the Instructor Companion Web site found at www.cengagebrain.com. It serves as an instructional resource and provides answers to coding exercises and test questions for content reinforcement.

EncoderPro.com—Expert 59-Day Free Trial

With the purchase of this textbook you receive free 59-day access to *EncoderPro.com—Expert*, the powerful online medical coding solution from OptumInsight©. With *EncoderPro.com—Expert*, you can simultaneously search across all code sets.

How to Access the Free Trial of *EncoderPro.com—Expert*

Information about how to access your 59-day trial of *EncoderPro.com—Expert* is included on the printed tear-out card bound into this workbook; the card contains a unique user access code and password. Once you log in, scroll down to the bottom of the License Agreement page, and click the "I Accept" link. Then, click the "I Accept" link on the Terms of Use page. Be sure to check with your instructor before beginning your free trial because it will expire 59 days after your initial login.

Features and Benefits of *EncoderPro.com—Expert*

EncoderPro.com—Expert is the essential code lookup software from OptumInsight© for CPT, HCPCS (level II), ICD-9-CM Vol. 1, ICD-9-CM Vol. 3, ICD-10-CM, and ICD-10-PCS code sets. It gives users fast searching capabilities across all code sets. *EncoderPro.com—Expert* can greatly reduce the time it takes to build or review a claim, and it helps improve overall coding accuracy.

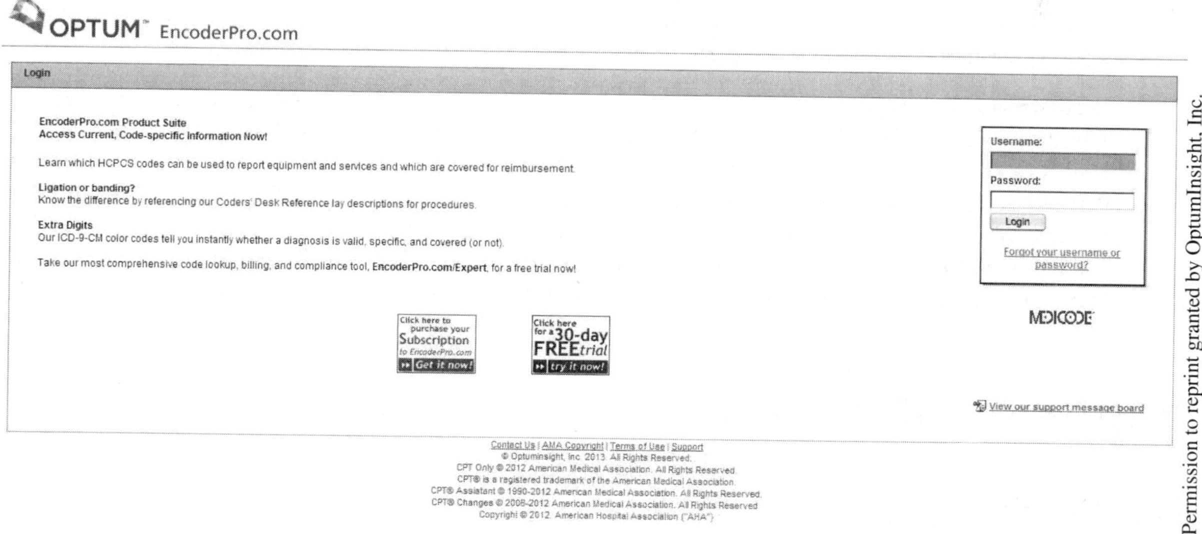

During your free trial period to *EncoderPro.com—Expert*, the following tools will be available to you:

- **Powerful CodeLogic™ search engine.** Search all code sets simultaneously using lay terms, acronyms, abbreviations, and even misspelled words.
- **Lay descriptions for thousands of CPT® codes.** Enhance your understanding of procedures with easy-to-understand descriptions.

- **Color-coded edits.** Understand whether a code carries an age or sex edit, is covered by Medicare, or contains bundled procedures.
- **ICD-10 Mapping Tool.** Crosswalk from ICD-9-CM codes to the appropriate ICD-10 code quickly and easily.
- **Great value.** Get the content from over 20 code and reference books in one powerful solution.

For more information about *EncoderPro.com—Expert* or to become a subscriber beyond the free trial, email us at **esales@cengage.com**.

Coding and Medical Insurance Policies

Coding can be significant in receiving and keeping payment for medical services. One publication states that coding makes a 25% greater or lesser difference in payment. It is the insurance policy language that defines payable benefits. Beginning coders may ask, "What code do I use to get paid?" A patient who has not received payment may say that the doctor reported the "wrong" code. The answer for both situations is clear. You always use the correct code.

Doctors often find coding confusing. They may do a new service that does not have a specific code. Do you report it with an existing code number? Sometimes the procedure is not really new, but the doctor uses a new technique or technology. Medicare, the Blues (Blue Cross/Blue Shield), or another payer may notify the doctors to report these services under another code. However, without specific instructions to call the service something different, you should report it under the "unlisted procedure" code. The "Instructions for Use of the CPT Book" emphasize this point by stating, "Do not select a CPT code that merely approximates the service provided. If no such procedure or service exists, then report the service using the appropriate unlisted procedure or service code." The insurer can decide to pay or reject the claim based on the terms of the policy.

Perhaps a new code is now available for a recently developed procedure. Unfortunately, the service may be too new to appear on the insurance policy benefit list and so the payer rejects the claim. The doctor now wonders if you should code it with last year's code. You may decide to make the change after offering explanations to the irate patient who now has a large, unexpected bill. In these no-win situations, it may seem easier to recode and rebill the service. Don't do it. Resist that temptation. The medical record does not support any code but the correct one.

Insurers match the claims with their benefit schedule. Medicare pays for few preventive services. Religious organizations may have policies that do not cover sterilizations or abortions. Payers then send the doctor or policyholder the specified payment or a rejection. If you change the code to make the service payable, it is fraud. Also, a service may not be payable for the diagnosis provided. Suppose the doctor sees a patient for bronchitis and notices that it is time to repeat the electrocardiogram (ECG) as the patient has a family history of heart disease. If the office bills the ECG with the diagnosis of bronchitis, the payer probably will reject the service. Taking an ECG is not a standard procedure for bronchitis. It is correct to report the office visit for bronchitis and the family history of heart disease for the ECG.

Some situations are less clear. No insurer would deny a person the reconstruction of his nose following a serious auto accident, a fall from a horse, or a similar incident. What if the injury occurred 10 years ago? Should the automobile insurer, the owner of the stable, or the patient's own insurance pay the doctor's bill? Is the patient's health insurance primary and expected to pay first before the other insurers? All these health insurance payment problems do not affect the determination of the correct diagnosis and procedure codes.

Medicare and private insurance are separate programs. Medicare's coding rules work, and the Health Insurance Portability and Accountability Act (HIPAA) requires health insurers to adopt the government-approved coding specifications of Medicare and Medicaid. However, Worker's Compensation and the auto insurance industry are exempt from HIPAA and may continue to use the older diagnosis coding system. If you work for a pediatrician, becoming aware of Medicare rules may be difficult. Pay close attention to payer bulletins and the information on coding distributed at their seminars and workshops. Many private organizations and medical specialty societies offer coding workshops. Try to attend one each year and always end the year with the purchase of new coding references.

Conquering Coding

You may be surprised by how much experience you have with coding. You use it every day. From social security, telephone, and credit card numbers, to thermometers and cable television selectors, numbers that represent words surround us. If you see $1.00, you think "one dollar." Even without a description or explanation, you probably recognize 1-800-555-1212.

Our present diagnosis coding system is ICD-9-CM, the *International Classification of Diseases, Ninth Revision, Clinical Modification*. Disease coding systems began in the late 1800s and identified the causes of death. The ICD system is now used worldwide to record the incidence of disease. Many ICD-9-CM reference books include this history. Take the time to read this fascinating summary of disease recording. ICD-9-CM is a three-volume reference, available from many sources at prices ranging from $19.95 to almost $200.00.

In the near future, we begin to code diagnoses in ICD-10-CM. The 2014 ICD-10-CM is still labeled "draft" as the first complete publication of ICD-10-CM is expected in 2015 or 2016. There has been no change in the structure of ICD-10-CM since the 2010 draft, but there have been many changes in the guidelines and the code sections have been expanded.

The American Medical Association (AMA) developed the procedure or service coding reference, *Current Procedural Terminology (CPT)*. This single volume reference is available from many sources, but the AMA carefully protects the copyright and printing of CPT.

The Health Care Financing Administration (HCFA), now named the Centers for Medicare and Medicaid Services (CMS), the agency responsible for Medicare and Medicaid, recognized that many medical services were not physician services. To report, pay, and monitor ambulance services, medical equipment, and supplies, another set of codes was needed. This system is called the *Healthcare Common Procedure Coding System* or HCPCS (pronounced "hick-picks"). HCPCS has two levels of codes, usually indicated by Roman numerals. The Level I codes are the CPT codes, five digits, or four numbers followed by a letter. Level II codes have a letter followed by four numbers. The Level III codes, or "local" codes were eliminated with the implementation of the HIPAA standardized code sets in October 2003.

Coding determines the appropriateness of treatment and the medical necessity for a service. Insurers compile statistics on the frequency of a service, sometimes identifying "abused" procedures. They state that many doctors do C-sections for their own convenience rather than patient need, for example. Monitoring the codes billed, Michigan Blue Shield found a physician who did almost half the endoscopic procedures reported in one year. A Medicaid program discovered a doctor who reported over 400 house calls in one day. The payers, like you, found these data unbelievable, audited the physicians, and recovered the overpayments.

Coding Ground Rules

1. Keep your coding references current. Purchase new books each year.
2. Know the coding rules and apply them properly.
3. Code only what the documentation supports.
4. Match the diagnosis code with the procedure code. They must be "reasonable."
5. Review and update all charge tickets, computer files, and encounter forms annually.

INTRODUCTION TO *CURRENT PROCEDURAL TERMINOLOGY (CPT)*

The American Medical Association (AMA) released the first edition of *Current Procedural Terminology (CPT)* in 1966. It was similar to a coding system called the California Relative Value System (CRVS) developed 10 years earlier by the California Medical Association (CMA). These codes were based on a four-digit system. In 1970, the AMA released the second edition of the CPT manual, adding a fifth digit to the codes to make services more specific. The third edition was printed in 1973 and the fourth edition in 1977. Also, during this time, many insurance companies developed their own coding systems. Some payers used these coding systems internally, and others required the doctor to use these special codes to report services to that insurer.

By 1983, a government study identified over 120 different procedure-coding systems. It was impossible to match services with all these different coding systems, so the government mandated a standard coding system for Medicare and Medicaid. Beginning in 1984, the government required physicians to report all services in HCPCS for all Medicare and Medicaid claims. Also in 1984, the AMA modified the name of the CPT manual and began including the year in the title of the publication.

CPT-1992 changed all the "visit" services, such as office calls, hospital care, and nursing home visits, to Evaluation and Management (E/M) services. In spite of many articles in medical publications, seminars, and newsletters, some physicians still have trouble determining the exact level of care to use for a patient visit. While deciding the correct level of service is the responsibility of the physician, not the medical assistant or biller, we will explore these codes in the worksheets. Medicare required this change as part of their implementation of the Resource Based Relative Value Scale (RBRVS) mandated by Congress to reform the Medicare payment structure.

The present edition of the CPT manual contains over 7,500 different descriptions of services. The AMA protects these codes and descriptions by a copyright. Look at the introductory pages of the current CPT edition where credit is given to the CPT Panel and Advisory Committees responsible for developing these codes. The Table of Contents of the CPT manual shows the organization of the references. Note that the largest section, as you would expect, is the Surgery listing. Appendix B of the CPT manual summarizes the code changes since the last edition. This list identifies the codes you must update in your computer or on office documents. Some CPT code book vendors and AMA have editions with color-coded pages, color keys, and thumb-indexed pages to make it easier to use. Their terminology and illustration sections can provide guidance with unfamiliar terms. The CPT manual's index is not complete, but it can help you search for many codes.

Most successful projects start at the beginning. Look at the CPT manual's Introduction. Many of the higher numbered codes, the E/M services, appear first since most physicians provide these services. A doctor can report a code from any section if that is the service performed. However, the reasonableness of the code must be tested. Would a podiatrist perform neurosurgery? Not likely, but it could appear that way if you transpose digits in the procedure code. Later, we will work with a worksheet that looks at reasonable code matching. The terminology format, with the stem of the procedure before the semicolon, saves space and makes the page easier to read. This code layout is standard in the CPT, HCPCS, and ICD-10-CM references.

Coding guidelines appear in each section of the CPT manual. You must read these carefully to select the correct codes in this workbook. Procedure descriptions may be misleading if you have not read the rules. We will review the "separate procedures" in the surgery section. The "modifiers" do just that; they modify or change a service. They are so important that all modifiers are listed in the CPT manual's Appendix A. Complete your reading of the CPT's Introduction and review any of the terminology and anatomy pages. Now you are ready to start the worksheets in this workbook.

Evaluation and Management Services

The first three worksheets of *2014 Coding Workbook for the Physician's Office* cover the basic medical visit services provided by almost every health care professional. These are the E/M codes. The service descriptions are complete but confusing. An understanding of terms is critical to accurate interpretation of the services. You must read the CPT definitions of commonly used terms carefully. If you are responsible for billing and have obsolete codes or descriptions on the office encounter or computer forms, change them immediately. You may find an old code or modifier in your computer system. Delete old codes only after making certain you do not need them for statistical use. Contact the vendor of your computer system or software to find the correct procedure for handling obsolete codes and modifiers.

There are three to five levels of many E/M codes. Encounter forms may have a cell labeled "New Patient" and code "99201" listed with the description "Level 1." The guidelines also advise you that the descriptions vary for all Level 1 codes. As you review the instructions, look at the codes used for illustration. The presenting problems, time, and face-to-face clarifications are essential components of the service descriptions. Review the instructions on selecting a level of E/M service with the doctors and other professionals so that the documentation in the patient's medical record matches the service level reported.

CPT Appendix C provides some clinical examples for each level of service. These are identified by specialty and may help you to select the correct code. Do not read anything into the case study that is not there. If we assumed that the patient was blind, obese, or had another complicating problem, the level of service might change. Base your interpretation on the information provided and nothing else.

Remember our earlier reference to policy benefits deciding whether a code would result in payment? The same rules affect modifiers. Medicare allows the modifier –21, prolonged E/M service, when applied to only the high-level codes. Other payers may not honor or may have special rules for using a specific modifier.

Following the guidelines section, CPT begins with the E/M codes. You will find explanatory information throughout the section. You must read these instructions. Many worksheet items use this additional material. The reformatted visit codes on the next page show the similarities and contrasts for these services. Some criteria are consistent for most codes. New patient services require all three key components: history, examination, and medical decision making. Established patient services need two of the three key components. The wording of the paragraph on counseling and coordination of care is consistent throughout the E/M codes.

The section covering the visit codes may be the most complex in CPT. From here it will become easier. Again, review the guidelines and other instructions carefully as they explain the components of each code. Code the worksheets of E/M encounters described in terms used by physicians, not the CPT committee. You may not agree with the level of the code listed on the answer sheet, but your choice should be from the same group of codes. Aren't we glad that choosing the appropriate level of E/M codes is the responsibility of the provider and not the coders? However, your knowledge of these codes can help the provider report the appropriate code for the service.

In 1995, the AMA and HCFA released the documentation standards for E/M services. These described the components of the medical history, and the number of body areas and organ systems that the doctor must examine and document for each level of service. In 1997, HCFA clarified this list by identifying the mandatory elements of the exam. The doctor supports a detailed new patient exam (99203) by documenting 12 to 17 exam items. The complexity of medical decision making is also explained. Be certain there is a copy of these criteria in your office so anyone creating medical records can follow these guidelines. All payers should accept this documentation standard, and the AMA may include it in future editions of CPT.

When the first three E/M services are placed next to each other, it is easier to see the similarities and differences among the codes:

New Patient—99201 (referred to as patient 1)	**New Patient—99202** (referred to as patient 2)	**New Patient—99203** (referred to as patient 3)
Office or other outpatient visit for the evaluation and management of a new patient, which requires these three key components:	Office or other outpatient visit for the evaluation and management of a new patient, which requires these three key components:	Office or other outpatient visit for the evaluation and management of a new patient, which requires these three key components:
• A problem-focused history	• An expanded problem-focused history	• A detailed history
• A problem-focused examination	• An expanded problem-focused examination	• A detailed examination
• Straightforward medical decision making	• Straightforward medical decision making	• Medical decision making of low complexity
Counseling and/or coordination of care with other physicians, other qualified health care professionals, or agencies are provided consistent with the nature of the problem(s) and the patient's or family's needs.	Counseling and/or coordination of care with other physicians, other qualified health care professionals, or agencies are provided consistent with the nature of the problem(s) and the patient's or family's needs.	Counseling and/or coordination of care with other physicians, other qualified health care professionals, or agencies are provided consistent with the nature of the problem(s) and the patient's or family's needs.
Usually, the presenting problem(s) are self-limited or minor. Typically, 10 minutes face-to-face are spent with the patient or family.	Usually, the presenting problem(s) are of low to moderate severity. Typically, 20 minutes are spent face-to-face with the patient or family.	Usually, the presenting problem(s) are of moderate severity. Typically, 30 minutes are spent face-to-face with the patient or family.

Name ______________________

Evaluation and Management–I (99201–99239)

2014 CPT Codes

These codes cover office and outpatient visits, hospital daily visits, and medical services for patients in hospital observation units. Most physicians use visit codes, and sometimes they make over 90% of the services performed by a doctor or other qualified health care provider.

Remember, some E/M services may require modifiers.

1. Discussion of medications with the patient admitted yesterday and with the patient's family just before patient left the observation unit 99217
2. Hospital visit, will discharge patient tomorrow 99231
3. First visit: 2:15 p.m. to 3:20 p.m., multiple complaints: meds for diabetes, arthritis, and hypertension reviewed and changed as patient has rash secondary to present combination; also fulgurated wart on left ring finger ____________
4. Brief visit with nurse to verify proper use of inhaler 99211
5. Six-month follow-up visit for patient in exercise 3 above 99213
6. First day in observation unit, patient collapsed at shopping mall and continues to have an irregular heartbeat ____________
7. Admission to hospital for Boy Scout with severe poison ivy ____________
8. Initial office visit for child with chicken pox ____________
9. Eight-year-old girl seen again for severe sore throat and fatigue ____________
10. Admission to ICU for 72-year-old male with massive cerebral hemorrhage, respiratory failure, and coma ____________
11. Hospital visit for patient with severe reaction (rash, vomiting) to x-ray study dye, medication prescribed ____________
12. Comprehensive follow-up counseling visit, emotionally upset over child's behavior and marital problems, 3:15 p.m. to 4:00 p.m. ____________
13. Forty-eight-year-old male admitted to hospital for chest pain and discharged the same day when all diagnostic studies were within normal limits ____________
14. Spent 20 minutes reviewing improved lab work and discussing results with the patient. Will reduce meds, may discharge from observation tomorrow ____________

Name ______________________

Evaluation and Management–II (99241–99340)

2014 CPT Codes

Consultations occur when one provider requests the *opinion* of another provider. The consultant may perform tests to establish the opinion or may initiate treatment, but the patient remains under the care of the requesting provider. If the consulting physician assumes part or all the care of the patient, it is a referral and not a consultation. A surgeon is usually not a consultant but is expected to take care of the patient's problem. The term *consultation* is sometimes misused, as when the patient *consults* with the doctor. This is reported as an office visit. Consultation codes have two subcategories: office or outpatient and inpatient. Medicare stopped paying consultation codes in 2010, citing misuse. There are also codes for Emergency Services, Critical Care, and Nursing Facility Services, as well as Domiciliary, Rest Home, and Custodial Care Services.

1. Office consult for high school senior with a knee injury that occurred during the homecoming game 99241
2. Comprehensive admission service for the transfer of a psychotic patient from an acute care hospital to a psychiatric residential treatment center 99304
3. Initial hospital detailed consult for male diabetic, had back surgery 3 days ago, has a severe urinary tract infection; procedure scheduled for this afternoon ____________
4. One hour in ER with 3-year-old attacked by pit bull, found unconscious with bruises and scrapes, and requires no suturing ____________
5. Annual nursing facility visit ____________
6. Brief inpatient consult to rule out abscessed tooth in post-delivery female ____________
7. ICU consult for female with cardiac arrest during gallbladder surgery now in a coma ____________
8. Office consultation for teenager with severe acne ____________
9. Visit to home for the developmentally disabled to see a new patient with recent onset of swelling in hands and feet ____________
10. Constant attendance, 1.5 hours critical care in ICU for a 15-year-old male, comatose after diving accident ____________
11. Office consult for 58-year-old patient with Alzheimer's and previous stroke now combative and incontinent ____________
12. One-hour discussion with family of an elderly patient being discharged from rehabilitation facility to son's home for aftercare ____________
13. Comprehensive ICU history or exam; transfer to surgeon if not improved in 24 hours ____________
14. Follow-up skilled nursing facility visit for patient with recent onset of mini-strokes (30 minutes) ____________
15. Contacts with family and staff of assisted living facility revising care plan based on recent laboratory studies (July: 22 minutes) ____________
16. Alzheimer's patient with urinary tract infection seen at foster care home ____________

Name ______________________

Evaluation and Management–III (99341–99499)

2014 CPT Codes

These codes are used to report home services, prolonged services, physician standby services, case management, team conferences, care plan oversight, preventive medicine, non face-to-face care, newborn/infant services, and miscellaneous care. They cover special or preventive services that may be excluded under some insurance policies. Be certain the codes you report accurately reflect the services performed so the insurer can appropriately pay or reject the claim. Some services may be payable only for certain diagnoses or in specified locations.

1. Follow-up house call for child recovering from the flu 99341
2. Extended follow-up in NICU, unstable 2-month-old infant 99472
3. Admission of premature newborn to NICU 99477
4. Injured 18-month-old infant transported to Children's Hospital, pediatrician in attendance for 55-minute trip ______
5. One-hour conference at day-care center with psychologist, nurse, and geriatric assessment staff, pending transfer of patient to long-term care facility. Patient not present. ______
6. Forty-five minutes of Internet evaluations over the weekend with an established patient not seen in the past month but now threatening suicide ______
7. Initial exam of infant born at home ______
8. NICU visit, 5-day-old infant now weighing 4,200 grams, will transfer to nursery tomorrow ______
9. New patient, annual exam for pilot, age 47 ______
10. Following an EPF visit (99282) in the ER for a 90-year-old patient, the physician spent another hour with the patient's spouse and children contacting long-term care facilities and a geriatric physician to develop a plan of care for the patient ______
11. Standby services (45 minutes) required for cesarean/high-risk delivery ______
12. Counseling on risk factors for sexually active 14-year-old female, 45 minutes ______
13. Preschool exam for 5-year-old child seen since infancy ______
14. Services for the month of June (25 minutes) supervising the hospice team for care of terminally ill cancer patient. Patient not seen. ______
15. Initial home visit to discuss care options with family of an 88-year-old disabled stroke patient, one hour ______
16. In-office initial management and monitoring of 47-year-old male on Coumadin, nine INR tests and subsequent dosage adjustment, second quarter ______

Name ____________________________

Anesthesia Services (00100–01999)

2014 CPT Codes

Physicians who are not anesthesiologists may report anesthesia services. A doctor may be responsible for the anesthesia when a partner performs a surgical procedure. Some large practices have their own surgery room, performing the same procedures in the office that they would do in the hospital outpatient surgicenter. In some cases, an anesthesiologist may not be available. Medical billers should become familiar with these codes and the rules for using them. These services may be a significant part of your coding work in the future.

Anesthesia use requires some special modifiers, P1 through P6 to indicate the patient's condition and some of the usual CPT modifiers. There are also some 99xxx codes that you bill along with the regular anesthesia service when there are qualifying circumstances. Keep these special rules in mind as you complete the worksheet.

The descriptions do not specify anesthesia, but all answers should come from this section. Watch for procedures that need a modifier or multiple codes.

1. Cervical diagnostic discography injection ______________
2. Abdominal repair, hernia of the diaphragm ______________
3. Delivery of twins, no C-section ______________
4. Radiation therapy requiring general anesthesia ______________
5. Total joint replacement, left ankle, for severe arthritis ______________
6. Tenoplasty, left shoulder to elbow ______________
7. Burr holes, critical newborn infant ______________
8. Dual chamber transvenous pacemaker insertion ______________
9. Rhinoplasty, correction of deviated septum ______________
10. Mid-thigh amputation, right leg ______________
11. Harrington rod implant, spinal cord biopsy ______________
12. Rectal endoscopy with biopsy ______________
13. Insert umbrella filter, inferior vena cava ______________
14. Pectus excavatum repair, 4-year-old male ______________
15. Arthroscopy, right shoulder ______________

General Surgery Rules

Surgical procedures on the integumentary system begin the extensive surgery section. CPT provides important guidelines for all surgeries. Review them carefully. Then consider the information below as you review the worksheet items.

1. Necessary medical care for diagnostic surgery may be reported separately. Nondiagnostic surgical services include concurrent medical care by the operating surgeon. Other physicians may report medical care that is unrelated to the surgical service. Example: A patient undergoing gallbladder surgery is followed by an internist for chronic emphysema. The internist is paid for the medical care not related to the surgical service. Medicare has comprehensive tables identifying, by procedure code, the days of medical care included in a surgical service. Other insurers may use the same list or have similar restrictions.
2. Surgical services usually include any local anesthesia administered by the operating surgeon.
3. The payment for the surgery includes all related supplies. The doctor may bill for supplies only if they exceed what is usually required for that service. Insurers may refuse to pay for any additional supplies provided by the surgeon. If the surgery is done in the hospital setting, either inpatient or outpatient, payers assume the hospital provided all the necessary supplies.
4. The subsection information contains the special instructions for using a particular range of codes. In some cases, this vital information may appear on the previous page. Always, after you find the code you seek, review the previous page or two for any special rules related to this coding section.
5. A service that is usually part of another service may, on occasion, be reported as the primary surgery. These codes appear throughout CPT and the description ends with "separate procedure." If you perform a service with the "separate procedure" notation, report that service if it is the *only* service performed or is unrelated to the other procedures or services performed. Use the modifier –59, Distinct Procedural Service, to indicate this service is unrelated to the other procedures or services reported. This is a rule many doctors and billers find confusing.
6. Surgical destruction is usually included in the primary procedure.
7. Use the unlisted procedure code at the end of each surgery section when there is no code for the service performed. New procedures are reported with these codes until a specific code is assigned. If the service involves a new technique for an established procedure, you would usually report the service with the existing code unless the technique is specified in the description. Note that all unlisted procedure codes end in "9" and many end in "99." Remember, whenever you report these unlisted services, you will need to make the operative notes available or provide a complete description of the service.
8. The special report is similar to the unlisted procedure. Again, you must explain the service completely. Documentation must be sent with the claim. These claims may not be accepted electronically as they require attachments. Some payers have a fax line to receive the required documentation for electronic claims.
9. Some of the CPT surgery modifiers may be listed in the guidelines of each surgery section. All CPT modifiers appear in CPT Appendix A.
10. Some complications may be reported in addition to the surgery using the modifier –22 and a detailed explanation. Medicare will usually reject any medical care billed by the surgeon during the specified postoperative period. To get paid, the surgeon must establish that the medical care rendered is not part of the usual postoperative care for the previous surgery.

11. Modifiers –54, –55, and –56 cover situations where the surgeon does not provide all the medical care related to the surgery. Physicians other than the surgeon may provide and be paid for medical care related to the surgery if the surgeon indicates his service does not include the preoperative or postoperative medical care.

12. Sometimes the doctor performs multiple procedures. If the surgery is a bilateral carpal tunnel release, you may be instructed by the payer to report the code and the modifier –50 or to report two identical lines, one with modifier –RT and the other with modifier –LT. Suppose the patient has gallbladder surgery and the doctor also removes nevi from the left neck and left thigh, and a basal cell CA of the scalp. You would report the major procedure on the first line, the basal cell CA on the second line, and the nevi on subsequent lines in the order of diminishing significance. The modifier –51 would be used on all but the first service line. Exception: See 14 below. Also, each service line must show the appropriate diagnosis code reference number.

13. Therapeutic surgery includes all related medical care. The modifier –24 is used when the surgeon performs a separate, postoperative medical service unrelated to the surgical procedure. Example: A patient had a surgery last week but now visits the surgeon's office for an acute asthma attack. If the asthma is unrelated to the surgery, the office visit may be billed as a separate service with modifier –24.

14. Some multiple surgical procedures must be reported without modifier –51. These are the "add-on" codes, identified in CPT Appendix D. Because these codes are added on to the reporting of another code, they can never be used alone. When printing paper claim forms, be sure that these codes do not roll over to be the only service on another claim form.

15. CPT Appendix E lists the CPT codes that are not "add-on" codes but do not require the modifier –51. Codes such as 20975 (electrical stimulation to aid bone healing, invasive, operative) or 31500 (intubation, endotracheal, emergency procedure) are billable but may be related to another reported service. Watch this Appendix closely if you perform these services as this list is updated yearly. Medicare rejects these codes as incorrectly reported if modifier –51 is attached.

Modifiers increase in importance every year. Each new edition of CPT and HCPCS bring changes in the familiar ones and new modifiers. Be certain you review the modifier sections when you look for changes in procedure codes.

Medicare and most other payers reject "unbundling," the reporting of multiple services when one code includes all procedures. When physicians code from a list, they may miss a code that contains multiple services. Encounter forms or coding sheets may state:

51840	Marshall-Marchetti
58150	Abdominal Hysterectomy
58700	Salpingectomy(ies)
58940	Oophorectomy(ies)

Turn to code 58150. The description includes codes 58700 and 58940. Suppose the patient with the abdominal hysterectomy also had a Marshall-Marchetti type procedure. The correct code, 58152, contains all the procedures listed above. The CMS rebundling list is called the "Correct Coding Initiative" or CCI, and is revised quarterly. Many insurance carriers implement these policies as soon as CMS releases them.

Caution: The CPT worksheets may require multiple procedure codes, a modifier, or the reporting of quantity. Any time the CPT code says "each," you need to report a quantity, even if it is only one. As you complete the worksheets, pronounce the terms. You can increase your vocabulary as you expand your coding skills.

Integumentary System

These codes include procedures on the skin, subcutaneous and accessory structures, nail, and breast. They cover the removal of lesions, suturing, plastic repairs, burn treatment, and other surgeries. Read the embedded instructions immediately under the headings "Removal of Skin Tags" and "Shaving of Epidermal or Dermal Lesions." Would we report suturing with the shaving of a dermal lesion? No, because the notation states that "the wound does not require suture closure."

Look at CPT's Rule 2 for Repair (Closure) when repairing multiple lacerations. Add together the length of all wounds in the same classification and report the total as a single item. This rule does not apply to excising multiple lesions, as each is reported individually. A ruler with both inches and centimeters will help you report the correct codes for lesions and suturing.

Before beginning the worksheets, look at the codes and read the text of the entire integumentary section. You may wish to have a medical dictionary and anatomy reference handy. Benign lesions are listed before malignant; suturing is simple, intermediate, and complex; and the miscellaneous categories list services that do not fit into other sections. The integumentary system ends with procedures on the breast.

Note: Watch for worksheet items requiring a modifier, quantity, or multiple codes.

Name ____________________

Integumentary System (10021–19499)

2014 CPT Codes

1. Hair transplant, 21 punch grafts ____________
2. Removal of eight skin tags from left forearm ____________
3. Removal of Norplant contraceptive capsules ____________
4. Simple blepharoplasty, right upper lid ____________
5. Reclosure, three surgical wounds ____________
6. Debridement of skin and subcutaneous tissue, left forearm ____________
7. Permanent removal distal half, left great toenail ____________
8. Full thickness graft 2 × 5 cm., left cheek ____________
9. Simple right shoulder biopsy, single skin lesion ____________
10. Adjacent tissue transfer, trunk, 8 sq. cm. ____________
11. Laser destruction, benign 2 cm. facial lesion ____________
12. Excision/Z-plasty repair, 11 sq. cm. forehead lesion ____________
13. Aspiration, breast cyst, right ____________
14. Burn site preparation of back, 4%, 9-year-old female ____________
15. Wound suture, 3/4″ right hand, 1/2″ left foot ____________
16. Breast reduction, left ____________
17. Excision, simple repair, right axillary hidradenitis ____________
18. Xenograft, left thigh, 4 × 8 cm. ____________
19. Excise malignant 1/2″ lesion, neck ____________
20. I&D (incision and drainage) hematoma, left hand ____________
21. Major debridement of partial thickness burns, both legs ____________
22. Mohs technique, seven tissue blocks, abdomen ____________
23. Leg fracture, open, debride left thigh, remove gravel, bone spicules ____________
24. Split autograft, back (2% body area), 2-year-old male ____________
25. Lipectomy, right buttock ____________

Musculoskeletal System

Three worksheets on the musculoskeletal system cover the largest unit in the surgery section. They describe procedures on the supporting structures of the body such as bone, muscle, and tendon. The first worksheet includes trauma, excision or removal, replantation, grafting, the head, neck and thorax, spine, abdomen, and shoulder. The second worksheet has procedures on the arm, hand and fingers, and pelvis and hip joint. The third involves services on the femur, knee, leg, ankle, and foot and concludes with casting, strapping, and arthroscopy.

The many rules and definitions appearing within the chapter give specific instructions on coding. Note that the service includes the first cast or traction device. This information is repeated at the start of the casting section. There are also modifiers to identify the service as right or left, and ones that identify specific digits.

Some doctors use the terms "closed" and "open" to describe both the fracture and the treatment. If this is happening in your office, talk to the provider and get the treatment clarified before billing the service.

The musculoskeletal system is arranged by body site, from the top down, from the center out. After the general procedures, it is organized:

1. Head
2. Neck and thorax
3. Back and flank
4. Spine
5. Abdomen
6. Shoulder
7. Humerus and elbow
8. Forearm and wrist
9. Hand and fingers
10. Pelvis and hip joint
11. Femur and knee joint
12. Leg and ankle joint
13. Foot and toes
14. Casts and strapping
15. Endoscopy or arthroscopy

Most body site sections follow this organization:

1. Incision
2. Excision
3. Introduction or removal
4. Repair, revision, reconstruction
5. Fracture or dislocation
6. Arthrodesis
7. Amputation
8. Miscellaneous

Note how many worksheet items in the musculoskeletal section contain the diagnosis. Always exercise caution when selecting the ICD-10-CM diagnosis for the terms included in the procedure description. Watch for items that need multiple procedure codes; right, left, finger, and toe modifiers; or quantity specified.

Name ____________________

Musculoskeletal System–I (20005–23929)

2014 CPT Codes

1. Percutaneous needle biopsy, right deltoid muscle ____________
2. Partial acromionectomy, left ____________
3. Wick monitoring, muscle compartment syndrome, right leg ____________
4. Four segment kyphectomy ____________
5. Injection service for left TMJ arthrogram ____________
6. LeFort II reconstruction, two autografts ____________
7. Removal of total right shoulder prosthesis for replacement ____________
8. Fracture of mandible, dental fixation, closed ____________
9. Maxillectomy, intra-extra oral osteotomy, for cyst ____________
10. Radical sternal resection with major bone graft for osteomyelitis (two codes) ____________
11. Remove external wire fixation under anesthesia ____________
12. Treat open fractures, two thoracic vertebrae ____________
13. Right shoulder arthrodesis, no graft ____________
14. Care of simple nasal fracture, no manipulation or stabilization ____________
15. Right total shoulder ____________
16. Reattachment of total amputation of right thumb tip ____________
17. Anterior osteotomy, discectomy, two thoracic vertebrae (two codes) ____________
18. Medrol injection, right hip ____________
19. Exploratory arthrotomy, left A-C joint ____________
20. Open treatment blowout fracture, transantral, right orbit ____________
21. Microvascular anastomosis, osteocutaneous flap, left great toe ____________
22. Custom prosthesis preparation, left ear ____________
23. Explore right chest, multiple gunshot wounds ____________
24. I&D deep soft tissue, osteomyelitic abscess, left buttock ____________
25. Exploration of fusion, lumbar spine ____________

2.W.

Name ______________________

Musculoskeletal System–II (23930–27299)

2014 CPT Codes

1. Open repair of left Dupuytren's contracture 26045
2. Hypothenar opponensplasty, right 26494. Rt
3. Open Bennett fracture with internal fixation, left 26665 Lt
4. Secondary flexor repair and graft, right no man's land
5. Synovial biopsy of right elbow by arthrotomy
6. Manipulation lunate dislocation, closed
7. Darrach procedure, left
8. Decompression fasciotomy, extensor, left wrist
9. Fracture left olecranon, internal fixation, open treatment
10. Right Z-plasty fasciectomy with release of 3rd and 4th IP joints (multiple codes)
11. Repair nonunion of left radius without graft
12. Treatment of traumatic left hip dislocation, no anesthesia
13. Flap repair, syndactyly, right 4th web space
14. Removal of recurrent ganglion, left wrist
15. Transmetacarpal reamputation, left first finger
16. Subfascial soft tissue biopsy, right forearm
17. Manipulation with pin, left epicondylar fracture
18. Closed manipulation MP dislocation left 4th finger, with anesthesia
19. Saucerization distal phalanx, left ring finger
20. Total hip replacement, right
21. Remove implant, revise arthroplasty, left wrist
22. Opposition fusion and graft, left thumb
23. Microvascular toe-to-hand transfer 2nd and 3rd toe to previous bone graft, left hand
24. Right femur, epiphyseal arrest by stapling
25. Reinsert ruptured left distal triceps tendon with graft

Name ____________________

Musculoskeletal System–III (27301–29999)

2014 CPT Codes

1. Right shoulder arthroscopy with lysis of adhesions ____________
2. Phalangectomy, left 3rd toe ____________
3. Exploration with synovial biopsy by arthrotomy, left knee ____________
4. Release of left tarsal tunnel ____________
5. Left knee arthroscopy, sewing needle removed ____________
6. Fracture right medial malleolus, closed, no manipulation ____________
7. Surgical correction with fixation, left patellar fracture ____________
8. Gastrocnemius neurectomy, left ____________
9. Heyman midtarsal capsulotomy, right ____________
10. Lengthening multiple bilateral hamstring tendons ____________
11. I&D hematoma, left ankle ____________
12. Repair of Risser jacket ____________
13. Fracture femoral shaft, open with screws, left ____________
14. Right Joplin bunion repair ____________
15. Repair of severed collateral ligament, right ankle ____________
16. Knock-knee osteotomy, left, before closure ____________
17. Lengthening, left Achilles tendon ____________
18. Plantar fasciotomy, left, by arthroscopy ____________
19. Goldwaite procedure for dislocating patella, right ____________
20. Manipulation right trimalleolar fracture ____________
21. Guillotine amputation, left tibia/fibula ____________
22. Application of right long arm splint ____________
23. Left sesamoid fracture, closed treatment ____________
24. Revision right long leg cast, walker heel applied ____________
25. Right great toe IP joint arthrodesis ____________

Respiratory System

From nosebleed and tonsillectomy to removal of a lung, this section covers procedures associated with the nose, sinuses, larynx, trachea, bronchi, lungs, and pleura.

In this system, we are introduced to endoscopy. Note that when a surgical or therapeutic endoscopy is performed, the appropriate sinusotomy, diagnostic endoscopy, and inspecting all sinuses code is included. This is another example of correct coding or bundling of services.

Name ____________________

Respiratory System (30000–32999)

2014 CPT Codes

1. Partial removal, left inferior turbinate ____________
2. Split cricoid laryngoplasty ____________
3. Endoscopy with A&P ethmoidectomy ____________
4. Closure nasoseptal perforations from cocaine use ____________
5. Bronchoscopy with laser destruction of lesions ____________
6. Open tube thoracostomy for empyema ____________
7. External arytenoidopexy ____________
8. Revision of tracheostoma ____________
9. Parietal pleurectomy ____________
10. Intranasal antrotomy, right ____________
11. Plastic repair closure of tracheostomy ____________
12. Intrathoracic tracheoplasty ____________
13. Tracheobronchoscopy through tracheostomy ____________
14. Direct laryngoscopy with biopsy, via microscope ____________
15. Surgical nasal endoscopy, polypectomy ____________
16. Secondary major rhinoplasty ____________
17. Removal of toy from nose, 2-year-old male, in office ____________
18. Pneumonolysis with packing ____________
19. Radical neck, partial laryngectomy for CA ____________
20. Unilateral sinusotomy, three sinuses, right ____________
21. Polypectomy, office surgery ____________
22. Empyemectomy ____________
23. Surgical endoscopy, repair sphenoid CSF leak ____________
24. Left thoracoscopy, with wedge resection ____________
25. Needle aspiration, left lung ____________

Cardiovascular System

This section lists the surgical procedures on the vascular and cardiac systems: the heart, veins, and arteries. The instructional introductory paragraphs refer to first-, second-, and third-order vessels and vascular families and the injection procedures for arteriography.

The Society of Interventional Radiology (SIR) distributes an excellent reference explaining the family trees of the vascular system. This manual is available on their Web site.

Excellent cardiovascular coding references are available from the American College of Cardiology or the CPT Reference Guide for Cardiovascular Coding, updated annually and available from the AMA.

Because surgery on the cardiovascular system usually represents major surgery, there are few codes identified as "separate procedure." Operations on the arteries and veins include the intraoperative angiogram. Aortic procedures include the sympathectomy, if performed. Diagnostic cardiac catheterization is in the Medicine section.

Review the extensive explanation of pacemaker and cardioverter-defibrillator services. Coronary bypass grafting, both venous and arterial, is complex and requires careful reading.

Caution: Watch out for worksheet item 3. Move slowly and carefully through this CPT section.

Name ______________________________

Cardiovascular System (33010–37799)

2014 CPT Codes

1. Short saphenous vein stripping, left leg ______________
2. Vein graft repair, left brachial artery ______________
3. Coronary bypass grafts, one venous and two arterial ______________
4. Direct repair of vertebral artery aneurysm ______________
5. Relocation of pacemaker pocket ______________
6. Percutaneous transcatheter removal of broken arterial catheter fragment ______________
7. Open atrial septostomy with bypass ______________
8. Insertion AV sequential pacemaker and electrodes ______________
9. Needle placement, left jugular vein ______________
10. Removal of implanted arterial infusion pump ______________
11. Pulmonary artery embolectomy without bypass ______________
12. Mitral valvotomy with bypass ______________
13. Cardiectomy with heart transplant ______________
14. Intracatheter AV shunt for dialysis ______________
15. Diagnostic arterial puncture ______________
16. Cut down venipuncture, newborn ______________
17. Splenorenal bypass, synthetic graft ______________
18. Percutaneous transluminal fem-pop atherectomy, left ______________
19. Direct repair of ruptured splenic artery aneurysm ______________
20. Intrauterine fetal transfusion ______________
21. Repeat pericardiocentesis ______________
22. Repair lacerated aorta with cardiopulmonary bypass ______________
23. Resection with commissurotomy for infundibular stenosis ______________
24. Ligation/repair patent ductus arteriosus, 19-year-old female ______________
25. Patch closure of ventricular septal defect ______________

Hemic and Lymphatic Systems—Mediastinum and Diaphragm

These combined, small sections include procedures on the spleen, bone marrow, stem cell services or procedures, lymph nodes and channels, mediastinum, and diaphragm.

Compared to the cardiovascular section, this one is easy.

Note how many services are "separate procedure." These services may be performed at the same time and setting of other major procedures and are not reported separately.

Name ______________________

Hemic and Lymphatic Systems—Mediastinum and Diaphragm (38100–39599)

2014 CPT Codes

1. Superficial needle biopsy of inguinal lymph node ____________
2. Complete right axillary lymphadenectomy ____________
3. Repair acute traumatic hernia of diaphragm ____________
4. Insertion of thoracic duct cannula ____________
5. Drainage of single lymph node abscess, left axilla ____________
6. Laparoscopic splenectomy ____________
7. Open excision of deep axillary node, right ____________
8. Radical retroperitoneal lymphadenectomy ____________
9. Lymphangiotomy ____________
10. Mediastinoscopy with biopsy ____________
11. Partial splenectomy for traumatic injury ____________
12. Superficial inguinofemoral lymphadenectomy ____________
13. Retroperitoneal staging lymphadenectomy ____________
14. Correct newborn diaphragmatic hernia, insert chest tube ____________
15. Needle bone marrow biopsy ____________
16. Suprahyoid lymphadenectomy, right ____________
17. Eventration of paralytic diaphragm ____________
18. Deep jugular node dissection × 3 ____________
19. Allogenic bone marrow transplant ____________
20. Injection for lymphangiography, bilateral ____________
21. Resection of benign neoplasm from mediastinum ____________
22. Staging, partial pelvic lymphadenectomy ____________
23. Excise left axillary hygroma, deep neurovascular dissection ____________
24. Repair ruptured spleen ____________
25. Total pelvic lymphadenectomy by laparoscope ____________

Digestive System

This system covers procedures on the lips, mouth, palate, salivary glands, pharynx, adenoids, tonsils, esophagus, stomach, intestines, appendix, rectum and anus, liver, biliary tract, pancreas, abdomen, peritoneum, and omentum as well as bariatric surgery and hernia repair.

This diverse section contains endoscopic procedures and refers to the related radiographic guidance, supervision, and interpretation services. Remember that surgical endoscopy includes diagnostic endoscopy.

There were many changes in this section in the 2014 CPT, and more are expected in 2015.

Watch for multiple codes and the items that require a modifier.

Name ____________________

Digestive System (40490–49999)

2014 CPT Codes

1. I&D peritonsillar abscess ____________
2. Flexible esophagoscopy with removal of FB ____________
3. Open Roux-en-Y bypass for obesity ____________
4. Fredet-Ramstedt pyloromyotomy ____________
5. Transanal hemicolectomy ____________
6. Commando glossectomy ____________
7. Initial inguinal hernia repair, 4-year-old male ____________
8. Transsacral proctectomy ____________
9. Rubber band ligature hemorrhoidectomy ____________
10. ERCP with pancreatic duct stent ____________
11. Stomal colonoscopy for hemorrhage ____________
12. Esophagogastroduodenoscopy, balloon dilation of obstructed outlet ____________
13. Staging laparotomy for Hodgkin's, with intraoperative tube jejunostomy ____________
14. Second stage, primary bilateral cleft lip repair ____________
15. Total arch vestibuloplasty ____________
16. Subsequent peritoneal lavage with imaging ____________
17. Rectal stricture dilation under general anesthesia ____________
18. Cholecystectomy with cholangiography ____________
19. Thoracic closure of esophagostomy ____________
20. Flexible sigmoidoscopy with biopsy ____________
21. Partial left lobe hepatectomy ____________
22. Salivary gland biopsy by incision ____________
23. Hepaticoenterostomy by U-tube ____________
24. Removal of dental implant, left mandible ____________
25. Plastic repair of pharynx ____________

Urinary System

This section includes the procedures on the kidneys, ureters, bladder, prostate, and urethra and also transplant services including the harvesting of the kidney. Urinary endoscopy and other procedures identify special bundling instructions.

Caution: Read the worksheet items carefully. "Urethra" and "ureter" can look similar in some forms of the words. Note the different codes for male and female.

One worksheet item has two possible codes. What else do you need to know to find the exact code?

Name ____________________

Urinary System (50010–53899)

2014 CPT Codes

1. Subsequent urethral stricture dilation, 27-year-old male ________
2. Transurethral resection of prostate, complete ________
3. Closure of traumatic kidney wound ________
4. Infant meatotomy ________
5. Cystourethroscopy, fulguration of 1.9 cm. tumor ________
6. Complete cystectomy, bilateral lymphadenectomy ________
7. Bowel anastomosis with ureterocolon conduit, right ________
8. Repair of ureterovisceral fistula ________
9. Needleless EMG anal sphincter ________
10. Subsequent dilation urethra, 21-year-old female, no anesthesia ________
11. Cystourethroscopy, steroid treatment of stricture ________
12. Suprapubic catheter bladder aspiration ________
13. Exploratory nephrotomy ________
14. Partial excision of left kidney ________
15. Excision of Cowper's gland ________
16. Sling procedure for incontinence, 43-year-old male ________
17. Ureterolithotomy, stone in upper third ________
18. Plastic repair of ureter stricture ________
19. Litholapaxy, 2.7 cm. calculus ________
20. Marshall-Marchetti-Kranz procedure ________
21. Cystometrogram ________
22. Injection procedure for chain urethrocystography ________
23. Percutaneous placement of ureteral stent ________
24. Bilateral pyeloplasty for horseshoe kidney ________
25. Laser vaporization of prostate with TURP ________

Male Genital System, including Intersex Surgery

These codes identify procedures on the penis, testes, epididymis, tunica vaginalis, scrotum, vas deferens, spermatic cord, seminal vesicles, and prostate.

Because there are only two codes, intersex surgery is included in this chapter.

Watch for the worksheet item that has two possible answers.

Name ____________________

Male Genital System, including Intersex Surgery (54000–55899)

2014 CPT Codes

1. Newborn clamp circumcision ____________
2. Traumatic partial amputation of penis ____________
3. Punch biopsy of prostate ____________
4. Bilateral hydrocelectomy ____________
5. Radical retropubic prostatectomy ____________
6. Urethroplasty, 3rd stage Cecil repair ____________
7. Electroejaculation ____________
8. Implantation of prosthetic testicle, left ____________
9. Bilateral vasectomy ____________
10. Chemical destruction of penile condyloma ____________
11. Exploration of scrotum ____________
12. Complex scrotoplasty ____________
13. Insertion of radioactive pellet in prostate ____________
14. One stage repair, perineal hypospadias with tube ____________
15. Radical orchiectomy, abdominal exploration ____________
16. Insertion of inflatable penile prosthesis ____________
17. Abdominal vesiculectomy, right ____________
18. Varicocelectomy with hernia repair ____________
19. Abdominal exploration for undescended testes, bilateral ____________
20. Plethysmography of penis ____________
21. Biopsy and exploration of epididymis ____________
22. Testicular biopsy via needle ____________
23. Bilateral venous shunt for priapism ____________
24. Complex prostatotomy for abscess ____________
25. Sex change surgery, male to female ____________

Female Genital System and Maternity

This section defines reproductive system procedures; procedures on the vulva, perineum and introitus, vagina, cervix and corpus uteri, oviducts, and ovaries; and in vitro fertilization. Also included are the maternity services related to delivery, antepartum, and postpartum care.

There are several options for endoscopy in this section. You may need to read the procedure notes before coding the vulvar surgery as simple, radical, partial, or complete.

Note the services included in the prenatal or antepartum care. The instructions state: "other visits or services within this time period should be coded separately." This means that if you see a maternity patient for the flu or a burn, and you code it as unrelated to the pregnancy, you may bill it as an additional service. Would you bill inpatient medical care for the time your patient is hospitalized for delivery? No, not for the usual care associated with delivery, but you could report additional care for other complications. Also, another physician following the patient for an unrelated difficulty, such as a cardiac problem, would bill for regular medical care as it is not related to the delivery.

Examine the instructions on partial prenatal care. Note that *abortion*, not *miscarriage*, is the correct term for an uncompleted pregnancy. Abortions may be spontaneous, incomplete, missed, septic, or induced.

Some worksheet items may require multiple codes or quantity indicators.

Name ____________________

Female Genital System and Maternity (55920–59899)

2014 CPT Codes

1. Removal of three small leiomyomata by laparoscopy ____________
2. Repair of rectovaginal fistula with colostomy ____________
3. Intrauterine embryo transfer ____________
4. Diagnostic amniocentesis ____________
5. Cervical LEEP biopsy, small electrode ____________
6. Tubal occlusion with ring ____________
7. Surgical treatment of second trimester missed abortion ____________
8. Cystocele/urethrocele repair ____________
9. Chorionic villus sampling by needle ____________
10. Laparoscopic excision of pelvic lesions ____________
11. Injection of dye for hysterosalpingogram ____________
12. Salpingectomy for ectopic pregnancy, by laparoscopy ____________
13. Vaginal delivery with tocolysis ____________
14. Vaginal excision, three uterine fibroids, 240 grams ____________
15. Cervical stump excision, repair of pelvic floor ____________
16. Vaginal hysterectomy, partial vaginectomy, enterocele repair ____________
17. Vaginal trachelorrhaphy ____________
18. Laser destruction of extensive vaginal lesions ____________
19. Complete pelvic exenteration ____________
20. Bilateral excision of ovarian cysts ____________
21. C-section delivery with postpartum care ____________
22. Tubal ligation, one day after delivery ____________
23. Fascial sling for stress incontinence ____________
24. Biopsy perineum, two lesions ____________
25. Hysteroscopy, lysis of adhesions ____________

Endocrine and Nervous Systems

Procedures on the thyroid, parathyroid, thymus, and adrenal glands; pancreas; carotid body; skull, meninges, and brain; spine and spinal cord; extracranial and peripheral nerves; and autonomic nervous system; as well as destruction by neurolytic agent, neuroplasty, and neurorrhaphy are included in this worksheet.

The nervous system surgery is categorized by approach, definitive surgery, and reconstruction services that may be performed by more than one surgeon. You may want to refer to an anatomy text for clarification of the complex neurosurgical procedures.

Caution: Worksheet items 6 and 23: don't forget modifiers and quantity where needed.

Name ______________________

Endocrine and Nervous Systems (60000–64999)

2014 CPT Codes

1. Subtotal thyroidectomy with radical neck dissection ____________
2. Transcranial orbital exploration, removal of bullet ____________
3. Intra-abdominal avulsion, vagus nerve ____________
4. Laminectomy and excision of intradural sacral lesion ____________
5. Single nerve graft, left arm, 4.5 cm. ____________
6. Injection procedure, lumbar discogram (L4–L5) ____________
7. Decompressive resection, single cervical vertebral body ____________
8. Remove and replace CSF shunt system ____________
9. Percutaneous stereotactic chemical lesion, trigeminal ____________
10. Excision of thyroid adenoma ____________
11. Paracervical nerve block for delivery ____________
12. Repeat subdural tap through suture, newborn ____________
13. Excision with graft of infected intradural bone ____________
14. Total removal of implanted spinal neurostimulator receiver ____________
15. Bone flap craniotomy for cerebellopontine tumor ____________
16. Suture thenar motor nerve, right hand ____________
17. Exploratory burr hole, supratentorial, bilateral ____________
18. Repair complex dural intracranial AV malformation ____________
19. Cervical hemilaminectomy/re-exploration and decompression ____________
20. Brain stem biopsy, transoral/split mandible approach ____________
21. Excision of carotid body tumor and artery ____________
22. Craniectomy for posterior fossa tumor ____________
23. Cable nerve grafts, 3 cm. right arm and 4.5 cm. left leg ____________
24. LeFort osteotomy with fixation, anterior fossa ____________
25. Cranioplasty for 6.5 cm. skull defect ____________

Eye and Ocular Adnexa

This section lists procedures on the eyeballs, cornea, iris, ciliary body, lens, vitreous, retina, eye muscles, bony orbit, eyelids, conjunctiva, and lacrimal system.

Note the distinction between ocular and orbital implants. There are many laser procedures for the eye. Removal of a cataract may include other services. The surgeon may do the lens implant as a single stage procedure at the time the cataract is removed, or later.

Since there are two eyes and two ears, the -RT and -LT modifiers are especially important in the next two sections.

Watch for add-on or multiple codes and modifiers.

Name ______________________

Eye and Ocular Adnexa (65091–68899)

2014 CPT Codes

1. Probe/irrigate left nasolacrimal duct under general ____________
2. One laser treatment session, three small retinal breaks, left ____________
3. Exploration left orbit, remove embedded nailhead ____________
4. Excise 0.75 cm. conjunctival lesion, left eye ____________
5. Reinsert ocular implant with conjunctival graft, right ____________
6. Revise operative site, right anterior segment ____________
7. Removal of posterior FB with magnet, left eye ____________
8. Left tarsal wedge excision for ectropion ____________
9. Peripheral iridectomy for glaucoma, left ____________
10. Correction of right surgical astigmatism by wedge ____________
11. External levator repair, right blepharoptosis ____________
12. Enucleation, insertion of muscle stabilized implant, left ____________
13. Repeat scleral buckling, old retinal detachment, left ____________
14. Excise lower lid chalazions, three left, one right ____________
15. Right corneal laceration repair with tissue glue ____________
16. Laser treatment of left vitreous strands ____________
17. Removal of right dacryolith ____________
18. Laser trabeculoplasty, right ____________
19. Discission of left secondary cataract by incision ____________
20. Total reconstruction, right upper lid ____________
21. Extracapsular phacoemulsification with lens implant, left ____________
22. Posterior fixation for strabismus, resect two horizontal muscles, right eye ____________
23. Single plug closure, right lacrimal punctum ____________
24. Bilateral antibiotic injection, anterior chamber ____________
25. Initial superior oblique strabismus surgery, left ____________

Auditory System

This section includes procedures on the external, middle, and inner ear, and the temporal bone. After the eye, coding the ear services seems easy.

Caution: One worksheet item needs an add-on code; most need modifiers.

Name ____________________

Auditory System (69000–69990)

2014 CPT Codes

1. Replace left temporal bone conduction device ____________
2. Bilateral otoplasty for severely protruding ears ____________
3. Total facial nerve suture and graft with operating microscope ____________
4. Repeat right mastoidectomy, now radical ____________
5. Excision of right external ear cyst ____________
6. Neurectomy, right tympanic membrane ____________
7. Postauricular middle ear exploration, left ____________
8. Simple mastoidectomy, right ____________
9. Semicircular canal fenestration, left ____________
10. Stapedotomy, repair of right ossicular chain ____________
11. Catheterize/inflate left eustachian tube, transnasal ____________
12. Right oval window fistula repair ____________
13. Facial nerve repair, medial/geniculate, left ____________
14. Left tube tympanostomy with Novocaine ____________
15. Subtotal amputation, right external ear ____________
16. Cochlear implant, right ____________
17. Excision polyp, left ear ____________
18. Remove FB left external ear, general anesthesia ____________
19. I&D of abscess, left external meatus ____________
20. Myringoplasty, right ____________
21. Left mastoidectomy with labyrinthectomy ____________
22. Excision of neoplasm, left temporal bone ____________
23. Mastoidectomy/tympanoplasty, reconstruct right ossicular chain ____________
24. Excision left extratemporal glomus tumor ____________
25. Routine cleaning of right mastoid cavity ____________

Radiology

The first worksheet of radiographic procedures covers the section on diagnostic radiology and imaging. It includes flat films of the head and neck, chest, spine, pelvis, and upper and lower extremities. These studies are the most common radiologic procedures performed in the physician's office if the practice has the appropriate equipment.

The second worksheet includes studies of the abdomen, gastrointestinal and urinary tracts, and gynecological and obstetrical services. It also includes diagnostic imaging of the heart, aorta and arteries, and veins and lymphatics. It concludes with transcatheter procedures, transluminal atherectomy, and other therapeutic procedures.

The third worksheet covers three sections. The first section, diagnostic ultrasound or *echo*, includes procedures for diagnosis and guidance. The second section, radiation oncology, provides codes for clinical treatment planning, delivery and management, hyperthermia, and brachytherapy. The last section, diagnostic nuclear medicine, has codes for the endocrine, lymphatic, gastrointestinal, musculoskeletal, cardiovascular, respiratory, nervous, and genitourinary systems, and therapeutic nuclear studies.

Radiology services, with 70000 codes, is one of the nonsurgical sections in CPT. This section has special instructions, unlisted procedure codes, and modifiers. The "supervision and interpretation" services correspond to many of the injection procedures in previous surgical sections. Many of the "S&I" codes are followed by a reference to the surgical part of the diagnostic service. The Interventional Radiology Coding Users' Guide is very helpful in explaining these services.

Many specialists perform S&I studies, not just radiologists. Note that a written report, signed by the doctor interpreting the study, is part of the service and may not be billed separately. Nuclear medicine, once limited to the hospital setting, is now part of some medical practices.

Remember that the service at the doctor's office is the global or complete service, both the professional and technical components. The same study performed at the hospital must be reported as the "professional component," as the doctor does not own the equipment. The facility reports the "technical component" to be paid for the equipment, staff, supplies, lights, and other expenses associated with the service. With few exceptions, when the place of service is 21 (inpatient), 22 (outpatient), or 23 (emergency department), the 7xxxx service will require the modifier –26.

Move slowly through this section, reading all instructions and definitions. If you are confused by words ending in *-gram* or *-graphy*, think of telegram and telegraphy. One is the result, the other the process.

Watch for items requiring modifiers or multiple codes.

Name ____________________

Radiology–I (70010–73725)

2014 CPT Codes

1. S&I arthrography, left knee ____________
2. Thoracic discography, S&I ____________
3. X-ray of right knee, four views ____________
4. CT of pelvis, with contrast ____________
5. Neck CT with and without contrast and additional sections ____________
6. Pelvis, two views ____________
7. X-ray left eye, no foreign body ____________
8. Scoliosis x-ray study of the spine ____________
9. Chest x-ray, one view ____________
10. Outpatient TMJ arthrography, supervision/interpretation ____________
11. Technician administered functional MRI ____________
12. Two views right 4th finger ____________
13. Cervical MRI, no contrast ____________
14. X-ray teeth, right upper, left upper and lower ____________
15. Two views cervical spine, outpatient ____________
16. Right leg x-ray, 2-month-old baby boy ____________
17. Bilateral fractured ribs, three views ____________
18. X-ray left elbow, PA and lateral ____________
19. Complete study left hip ____________
20. Neck MRI, no contrast, inpatient ____________
21. X-ray exam left scapula, three views ____________
22. CT thoracic spine with contrast ____________
23. Proton imaging for lymph nodes, chest ____________
24. X-ray right sialolith ____________
25. Cervical myelogram S&I ____________

Name ______________________

Radiology–II (74000–76499)

2014 CPT Codes

1. Upper GI exam with delayed films and KUB ____________
2. Bilateral selective adrenal venography, S&I ____________
3. Videography of swallowing ____________
4. Acute abdomen series ____________
5. Cineradiography in operating room ____________
6. Bilateral selective adrenal angiography, S&I ____________
7. Supervise/interpret voiding urethrocystography ____________
8. Bilateral femoral intravascular ultrasound ____________
9. Transluminal balloon renal angiography, S&I ____________
10. LeVeen shuntogram, S&I ____________
11. Barium enema, KUB study ____________
12. Contrast monitoring to change percutaneous drain tube, S&I ____________
13. S&I retrograde brachial angiography ____________
14. Retrograde urography with KUB ____________
15. Percutaneous transhepatic portography, S&I, in ER ____________
16. S&I, hysterosalpingogram ____________
17. Supervise/interpret AV shunt angiogram ____________
18. Fluoroscopy, 50 minutes by non-operating physician ____________
19. Thoracic aortography by serialography, S&I ____________
20. Perineogram ____________
21. Lymphangiography, right arm, S&I ____________
22. Consult/report on x-rays done at University Hospital ____________
23. Transhepatic percutaneous cholangiography, S&I ____________
24. Follow-up CT study, localized ____________
25. Cardiac MRI and stress imaging with and without contrast ____________

Name ____________________

Radiology–III (76506–79999)

2014 CPT Codes

1. Complete obstetrical B-scan, 18 weeks, twin pregnancy 928 76805-76
2. Thyroid, metastatic CA imaging, total body, inpatient 920 78018
3. Simulation treatment planning, right hip and knee ____________
4. SPECT cardiac rest and exercise studies at hospital ____________
5. Lymph gland imaging ____________
6. Voiding cystogram reflux study with residual bladder study ____________
7. Radiation treatment: left shoulder and hip, 7.5 MeV ____________
8. Pulmonary ventilation and perfusion study ____________
9. Transrectal echo ____________
10. Intracavitary element placement, 11 ribbons, outpatient ____________
11. Combined B-12 absorption study ____________
12. Radioelement placement, surface of left forearm ____________
13. Ophthalmic biometry A-scan ____________
14. External hyperthermia, 2.7 cm. deep ____________
15. Splenic red cell survival measurement ____________
16. First pass cardiac resting study ____________
17. Brachytherapy planning, two sources ____________
18. SPECT bone imaging, professional component only ____________
19. Radiopharmaceutical treatment via joint infusion ____________
20. Ultrasound guidance for needle biopsy, S&I ____________
21. Radiopharmaceutical localization, lung abscess ____________
22. Neutron radiation, one area ____________
23. Repeat fetal Doppler echocardiogram ____________
24. Ultrasound guidance for amniocentesis, S&I ____________
25. SPECT liver imaging ____________

Pathology and Laboratory

Lab worksheet Part I covers lab panels, drug testing, therapeutic drug assays, evocative/suppression testing, clinical pathology consultations, urinalysis, and ends with chemistry tests. Note that the chemistry tests are listed in alphabetic order.

Part II includes molecular diagnostics, hematology, coagulation, immunology, and tissue typing. CPT 2014 had many changes in Molecular Pathology and Multianalyte Assays, codes 81200-81599, reflecting the new technologies used to detect variants in genes and/or DNA.

The final lab worksheet describes transfusion medicine, microbiology, anatomic pathology, including postmortem examination and cytopathology, cytogenics, surgical pathology, and miscellaneous laboratory services, ending with reproductive medicine procedures.

Reimbursement varies widely for laboratory studies. Review the manuals for the office testing equipment to determine the correct code for each study. Do not take the word of the equipment salesperson.

A federal regulation, the Clinical Laboratory Improvement Act (CLIA), rated laboratory tests by complexity. Each lab is certified to perform a specified level of testing. Some physicians discontinued all office laboratory work. Other practices reduced their laboratory work to only basic, uncomplicated services.

Because many lab tests are expensive, some laboratory order systems show the cost of the test being ordered. This helps the provider decide if the information gained from this study will be worth the cost.

As you complete the worksheets, review the guidelines, and look for instructions within each subsection. A few codes include the physician's services. Watch for the lab tests with legal implications. Unlike the surgical services, the clinical laboratory tests may be numbered so that the lowest code number identifies the most comprehensive study. A few describe testing you can do safely at home.

Some worksheet items require multiple codes or quantity reporting. Watch out for "qualitative" and "quantitative" as some tests have different codes for each study.

Name ____________________

Pathology and Laboratory–I (80047–83887)

2014 CPT Codes

1. Four studies each, luteinizing hormone and FSH ____________
2. Quantitative theophylline screen, blood ____________
3. Occult blood in stool, three guaiac test cards for neoplasm screen ____________
4. Qualitative cystine/homocystine, urine ____________
5. Urinary amino acids, quantitative, three specimens ____________
6. Glucose tolerance test, four specimens ____________
7. Blood ethanol levels ____________
8. Full sequence analysis BRCA1 and 2 ____________
9. Atomic spectroscopy, manganese ____________
10. HDL cholesterol direct measurement ____________
11. Manual microscopic urinalysis ____________
12. Blood catecholamines ____________
13. Creatinine clearance ____________
14. Obstetric panel of tests ____________
15. Hemoglobin, methemoglobin, qualitative ____________
16. Folic acid RBC ____________
17. Cocaine drug screening, qualitative ____________
18. Estriol ____________
19. Color pregnancy test, urine ____________
20. Total serum cholesterol ____________
21. Hepatitis A, B, C antibodies, B surface antigens ____________
22. Fractionation (17-KS) ketosteroids ____________
23. CRH stimulation panel ____________
24. Mucopolysaccharide screen ____________
25. TSH panel, four studies, 2 hours ____________

Name ______________________

Pathology and Laboratory–II (83915–86849)

2014 CPT Codes

1. Total blood protein, Western Blot 84181
2. Quantitative D-dimer degraded fibrin 85378-
3. PKU blood test, 2-day-old infant ________
4. Routine prothrombin time ________
5. Vitamin E ________
6. Total T cell with absolute CD4 and CD8 and ratio ________
7. Antibody detection for herpes simplex ________
8. Eastern equine encephalitis antibody test ________
9. Clotting factor VIII, single stage ________
10. Vitamin B-2 ________
11. C-reactive protein ________
12. Parathyroid hormone ________
13. Heparin neutralization ________
14. HLA typing, A, single antigen ________
15. Strip test, urea nitrogen ________
16. Skin test for histoplasmosis ________
17. Chorionic gonadotropin, qualitative ________
18. Hepatitis C antibody ________
19. Total testosterone ________
20. Platelet antibody identification ________
21. Urinary potassium ________
22. Total clotting inhibitor, protein S ________
23. Blood/urine Xylose absorption test ________
24. Rubella antibody screen ________
25. Double-strand DNA antibody ________

Name ____________________

Pathology and Laboratory–III (86850–89398)

2014 CPT Codes

1. Platelet pooling ____________
2. Bone marrow tissue analysis for malignancy ____________
3. Diagnostic scanning electron microscopy ____________
4. Stool culture for *Salmonella* ____________
5. Coroner ordered autopsy ____________
6. Surgical pathology, gross/micro, uterus with tumor ____________
7. Flow cytometry, DNA analysis ____________
8. Rabbit inoculation, observation ____________
9. Influenza detection by immunoassay ____________
10. Gross autopsy, including brain ____________
11. Surgical pathology, gross/micro cholesteatoma ____________
12. Preoperative autologous blood collection/storage ____________
13. Motility, volume and count semen analysis ____________
14. Consult/report on slides from University Hospital ____________
15. Antibiotic sensitivity study, 10 disks ____________
16. Chlamydia culture ____________
17. Limited chromosome analysis/banding, amniotic fluid ____________
18. KOH skin slide prep ____________
19. Forensic cytopathology for sperm ____________
20. CSF cell count with differential ____________
21. Thawing fresh frozen plasma, two units ____________
22. Immunofluorescent detection Type 1 Herpes ____________
23. Preparations for nerve teasing ____________
24. Collection of vaginal smear for dark field exam ____________
25. Intraoperative consultation and frozen section, two specimens ____________

Medicine

Worksheet I covers injections, psychiatry, dialysis services, diagnostic medical services for gastroenterology, and nonsurgical procedures on the eye and ear.

Worksheet II has cardiovascular and pulmonary diagnostic and therapeutic services, procedures for allergy, and neurology.

Worksheet III includes genetics, chemotherapy, and physical medicine. The special services of osteopaths and chiropractors, additional anesthesia codes, and other special procedures and services are the final subsections of CPT. The Category II and III codes may not be accepted by all insurance plans. Some of the special services, procedures, and reports also may be excluded from payment.

Many CPTs ago, office visits were part of the Medicine section. Then they became E/M services and are now listed separately. The invasive procedures in this section are diagnostic and are usually considered nonsurgical. This may seem strange since coronary angioplasty, the procedure some people have instead of open-heart surgery, is in this section.

Many doctors use services from this section, such as injections, EKGs, and pulmonary function testing. Generally, as you can see from the subsection listing, these services belong to a medical specialty. Study these services carefully. The guidelines for this section should be familiar. Now we apply them to medical services rather than surgery.

Caution: Watch for multiple codes, modifiers, and quantity reporting. One item requires a code from the E/M section.

Name ____________________

Medicine–I (90281–92700)

2014 CPT Codes

1. Anterior endothelial microscopy, cell count, photo/report 92286
2. Medical hypnotherapy to stop smoking 90880
3. One mini IM dose Rho(d) ____
4. Tinnitus assessment, right ear ____
5. Rhinomanometry ____
6. Binaural hearing aid exam ____
7. Manometric studies, anus and rectum ____
8. Bernstein test for esophagitis ____
9. Tangent screen visual fields, right eye ____
10. Supply Tetanus vaccine for use with jet injector, 27-year-old male ____
11. Hepatitis B immunization series, first visit, 19-year-old dialysis patient ____
12. Biofeedback training for arrhythmia ____
13. Monthly dialysis monitoring, 16-year-old female, one visit ____
14. Insight-oriented psychotherapy, 1 hour and 5 minutes, in the office ____
15. Psychotherapy with family, patient absent ____
16. Comprehensive eye exam, new patient ____
17. Fluorescein multiframe angiography, complete ____
18. Contact lens replacement, right ____
19. Impedance tympanometry ____
20. Start of dialysis training, one session ____
21. Air audiometry ____
22. Fitting of bifocal lenses ____
23. Electroconvulsive treatment, one session, for seizures ____
24. Audiometry by select picture ____
25. Inpatient nonverbal psychotherapy with medical visit, 45 minutes ____

Name ____________________

Medicine–II (92920–96020)

2014 CPT Codes

1. Coronary thrombolysis by IV infusion 92977
2. Inpatient right and left heart cath, congenital heart defect 93531
3. Interp/report only, tilt table cardiac testing ____________
4. Pulmonary percutaneous balloon valvuloplasty ____________
5. EMG cranial nerve supplied muscles, bilateral ____________
6. Dispense 15 doses antigen, bee and wasp ____________
7. Brief study, transcranial Doppler ____________
8. Cardiac stress test, tracing only ____________
9. Awake/sleep EEG, 10 p.m. to 7 a.m. ____________
10. CPAP ____________
11. Scratch tests, 10 trees, three venom ____________
12. Electromyography, 10 muscles, while running on treadmill ____________
13. Twenty-four-hour ECG, recording only ____________
14. Complete service, 1 month patient activated spirometry recording ____________
15. Repeat analysis of cranial nerve stimulator implant ____________
16. Myasthenia gravis challenge test ____________
17. His Bundle recording ____________
18. Complete four extremity plethysmography ____________
19. Venous Doppler, both legs, complete study ____________
20. Transesophageal echocardiogram, total service ____________
21. Ear oximetry for O_2 saturation ____________
22. S&I for ventricular angiography during left heart cath ____________
23. Stress echocardiogram, complete ____________
24. Complete ambulatory blood pressure monitoring, 32 hours ____________
25. Electrical testing of blink reflex ____________

Name ______________________________

Medicine–III (96040–0339T)

2014 CPT Codes

1. Nurse visit to patient's home for urinary catheter change ____________
2. Poisoning treatment with Ipecac, observation ____________
3. Iontophoresis, 30 minutes ____________
4. Limited developmental testing with report ____________
5. OMT, head and neck ____________
6. IV conscious sedation, 30 minutes, 67-year-old male, for esophageal dilation ____________
7. Phone evaluation, 25 minutes with suicidal patient who just returned from 2 months in Europe ____________
8. Acupuncture, four needles ____________
9. Documented assessment for risk of falls ____________
10. Breath test for rejection of heart transplant ____________
11. Telogen/antigen counts on hair clipped at the lab ____________
12. Assessment to determine suicide risk ____________
13. Behavior intervention, 30 minutes, twins and both parents ____________
14. Three hours medical testimony ____________
15. Initial nurse visit for infant born at home ____________
16. Scalpel wound debridement, 14.5 sq. cm. ____________
17. Reevaluation of physical therapy treatment ____________
18. Diabetic meal planning education, one hour, four patients ____________
19. Home visit and enema for fecal impaction ____________
20. Patient education/counseling, prescribed beta-blocker medication ____________
21. Chemotherapy, arterial infusion, 55 minutes ____________
22. Gait and stairs retraining, 30 minutes ____________
23. IM chemotherapy administration ____________
24. Chiropractic treatment, two spinal areas ____________
25. Home visit infusion, 5-year-old male hemophiliac, 1.5 hours. ____________

HCPCS LEVEL II CODES

Developed by the federal government, HCPCS (Healthcare Common Procedure Coding System) National Level II codes identify over 5000 codes and descriptive terminology for services not included in CPT. HCPCS provides codes for reporting supplies, injectables, and the services of nonphysician providers such as ambulance companies and Medicaid programs. HCPCS code changes start on January 1 with the new CPT codes.

Level II HCPCS codes begin with a letter followed by four digits. Although the codes were originally designed for Medicare and Medicaid, they are part of the HIPAA-designated code sets and most private insurers accept and understand them. Medicare, Medicaid, and some other payers may require the provider to register as a Durable Medical Equipment (DME) supplier before payment can be made for some supplies and equipment.

HCPCS lists codes alphabetically. Some Level II sections are unusual. D (dental) codes were eliminated in 2012 at the request of the American Dental Association. K codes are used only by Durable Medical Equipment Medicare Administrative Contractors (DME MACs) and are temporary codes. Many M (medical) services eventually appear in CPT so this list changes each year. Q codes are temporary codes, sometimes appearing mid-year when it becomes necessary to identify a service previously included in or reported by another code. Medicare and Medicaid bulletins will tell you when to report a new Q code. S codes may be used by the Blues, Medicaid, and commercial payers to facilitate claims processing and are not valid for the Medicare program. Medicaid programs asked for the inclusion of the T codes that may also be used by private insurers, but never for Medicare.

Read the introduction for an explanation of the HCPCS reference. Each of the sections begins with guidelines on how to use the codes correctly. There may be a mini-index to that section. The HCPCS index may show a single code, a range of codes, or provide no listing for that service. Like the CPT index, you may need to think of other ways to describe the service if you are to find the correct code.

HCPCS modifiers appear in the appendix or near the front or back of the book. Another appendix contains a summary of code changes. A different appendix has a list of modified or deleted codes. There are two sorted lists in HCPCS, a table of drugs, and a general index. Many private companies print versions of this codebook. Your reference may have numbers or letters to identify each appendix, or differ in format, but the codes and descriptions should be consistent with all vendors. These companies may also provide an expanded index or additional information on the use of these codes.

As you code the worksheet, start with the index. Then verify the code(s) with the actual code section as there may be sizes, quantities, or other variables in selecting the correct code. Read the guidelines to be certain you select the proper code. Many terms are similar and may be unfamiliar. If you use these codes in your work, consult with your employer to be certain you report the correct code.

HCPCS has special alphanumeric or two-letter modifiers. Some of these are included in the Modifier worksheet.

Name ______________________

HCPCS Level II Codes

2014 HCPCS

1. Delivery of monaural behind-the-ear hearing aid ____________
2. Medicaid case management, 1 month ____________
3. Injection, 100,000 units of Bicillin CR ____________
4. Premolded removable metatarsal support, right foot ____________
5. Chelation therapy ____________
6. Wellness assessment by a nurse practitioner ____________
7. Right shoe modified with outside sole wedge ____________
8. Dispensed 60 days of prenatal vitamins ____________
9. Injection, 8 mg Compazine ____________
10. Preschool screening for language problems ____________
11. Vinyl urinary bag with tube and leg strap ____________
12. Custom made plastic artificial eye ____________
13. Obtained Pap smear, sent to lab ____________
14. Methotrexate, 50 mg ____________
15. Non-emergency transportation by wheelchair van ____________
16. Nasogastric tubing, no stylet ____________
17. Adjustable aluminum three-prong cane, with tips ____________
18. Non-sterile dialysis gloves, one box of 100 ____________
19. Mitomycin, 5 mg injected ____________
20. Took x-ray machine to nursing home, one patient seen ____________
21. Hook hand prosthesis, closing ____________
22. Injection, Estradiol, 9 mg ____________
23. Needleless injection device ____________
24. Toronto orthosis for Legg Perthes disease ____________
25. Recording apnea monitor, high-risk infant ____________

Modifiers

Modifiers are two-character suffixes for procedure codes. They provide important information on how that service changed in some way without altering the definition of the code. Using modifiers properly eliminates some of the need to send procedure notes with claims. All CPT modifiers are two-digit numbers, and HCPCS modifiers are two letters or a letter and digit. Some modifiers apply to evaluation and management services only while others clarify surgical procedures. Both CPT and HCPCS provide a complete list of modifiers in an appendix.

CPT modifiers may indicate a reduced or expanded service, bilateral procedures, or the professional component of a service. HCPCS modifiers may indicate the rental or purchase of a piece of equipment, services by a social worker, or the services that are provided in a medically underserved area. Medicare and Medicaid may also direct you to apply HCPCS modifiers to CPT codes. Like the codes they modify, modifiers may be changed or eliminated with each new edition of CPT and HCPCS.

Modifiers may be shown as –22 or –AN. The "–" is not reported but is useful if you write out a code as "12345–22" or "54321–LT." The claim form and computer files have special columns or fields for modifiers. Some payers may ask you to report modifiers as a five-character code, 09922 or 099LT.

The worksheet requires a modifier for each scenario. Use the appendix in the CPT and HCPCS codebooks to select the correct two-character modifier. Some items may require multiple answers.

Name ____________________

Modifiers

2014 CPT

1. The patient had major surgery by Dr. Jones on July 16 and saw the doctor on August 4 for an unrelated office visit. The August 4 service requires modifier: ____________
2. Dr. Brown asks Dr. White to assist at a major surgery because a surgery resident is not available. Dr. White reports the surgery code with modifier: ____________
3. When an insurer requires a presurgical second opinion, the service is reported with the modifier: ____________
4. The surgery was difficult because the patient was a paraplegic weighing 427 pounds. To report these circumstances to the insurer, use modifier: ____________
5. Dr. Gray, the family doctor, asks a surgeon Dr. Green to see Mrs. Brown at City Hospital as she may need surgery. Dr. Green schedules the surgery for tomorrow and reports today's service with modifier: ____________
6. Dr. Thomas does an appendectomy and removes a mole from the patient's neck while in the OR. Use modifier ___ on the ___ service line of the claim form. ____________

2014 HCPCS

1. Dr. Reed, a clinical psychologist, saw a Medicare patient for diagnostic testing. Dr. Reed reports the service with modifier: ____________
2. If you refile a claim and change the procedure code because it was incorrect on the original claim, use modifier: ____________
3. When a procedure is recorded and stored on an analog tape recorder, use modifier QT. For a digital recording, use: ____________
4. Dr. Johns owns the portable x-ray equipment, but Dr. Hopkins does the interpretation and report. Identify the modifiers for both doctors: ____________
5. Dr. Little sees patients in an inner-city clinic designated as a physician scarcity area. He receives additional compensation for these services by reporting modifier: ____________
6. Mr. Small obtains a cane from the medical supply store. If it was a new cane, report modifier: ____________

INTRODUCTION TO ICD-10-CM

Diagnosis coding systems are older than procedure coding methods. More than 100 years ago a French physician developed a system for coding causes of death. In the early 1900s, the U.S. Public Health Service (PHS) began using the same codes. The World Health Organization (WHO) developed ICD in the late 1930s. In 1950, the PHS and the Veterans Administration (VA) adopted ICDA-8, the *International Classification of Diseases, Eighth Revision, Adapted.* With the U.S. implementation of ICDA-8 (ICD Adapted), our information on mortality and morbidity could be matched with statistics from the rest of the world.

Nongovernmental hospitals began to use ICDA-8, and the PHS expanded the system to include codes for surgery and treatment. Private agencies were also developing coding structures and by the 1960s, the United States used at least two diagnosis coding systems. In 1979, the government mandated the use of a new system, ICD-9-CM, for reporting services to Medicare and Medicaid and later extended to all payers by the Health Insurance Portability and Accountability Act (HIPAA).

The ICD-9-CM, *International Classification of Diseases, Ninth Revision, Clinical Modification*, was compatible with the WHO system, ICD-9. Congress required a standardized coding system for the implementation of Diagnosis Related Groups (DRGs), in 1983. The DRGs became part of Medicare's hospital inpatient payment method. All the diagnoses in ICD-9-CM were grouped into fewer than 500 DRGs. The hospital received payment for the inpatient's DRG category, not the cost of the patient's care.

After the government standardized the diagnosis coding system, many private organizations started printing the books with improvements. Some placed a color-coded box over the numbers that need a fourth or fifth digit; some distributed the codes in a ring binder; others had anatomical drawings throughout to illustrate the codes. You could buy a loose-leaf subscription for updated pages from some agencies. The government maintained the codes but no longer printed an annual edition of ICD-9-CM. However, the government does warn that it is not responsible for the errors made by others in printing the codes.

ICD-9-CM updated codes quarterly, but if the office bought a new book each August, it should be safe to use for the next year. The publishers print the year prominently on the cover so you know when the book becomes obsolete. It seems likely that the 2014 edition of ICD-9-CM will be the last one published now that ICD-10-CM will soon become the diagnosis coding system.

Many physicians' offices have used only 50 to 100 diagnosis codes. Rather than look them up each time, codes appear on encounter forms or "cheat sheets" used by the billers. There are two problems with this approach. First, the list restricts the number of diagnoses available. Do all the patients have only two or three kinds of anemia?

The worksheets contain columns for both ICD-10-CM and for ICD-9-CM. You will need access to the 2014 draft of ICD-10-CM manual to complete these exercises.

Using ICD-10-CM

The office may code either the principal diagnosis or the primary diagnosis for the patient visit. The principal diagnosis is the condition found after study. The primary diagnosis is the reason for the visit. Suppose you see a patient complaining of abdominal pain. If you can establish the cause, such as acute appendicitis, you may report that code. If the complaints are vague, maybe the flu, the threat of layoffs at work, or an upcoming week of final exams the doctor may code "abdominal pain" for the office visit. Hospitals must use the principal diagnosis on their claims.

While using CPT, we find a few services described by a person's name, an eponym. A medical term or anatomical description identified most procedures. One exception to this rule is bunion surgery where proper names are used to differentiate surgical techniques, such as Mitchell, Keller, McBride, etc. Diagnoses frequently use a person's name: Parkinson's or Cushing's disease, or a Bennett fracture. This is probably because the diagnosis coding system is older and diseases were traditionally named after the physician first reporting the condition.

As you do with CPT, you will need to become familiar with the diagnosis coding conventions. The medical office should observe the rules on "includes" and "excludes," but we may have limited use for the "code also underlying disease" if it is not specified in the medical record. Before beginning the worksheets, take time to review the introduction, the terminology, and the format of the alphabetic and tabular indexes. Also, pay careful attention to the ICD-10-CM Official Guidelines for Coding and Reporting and the chapter-specific coding guidelines.

Diagnosis Coding—Quick and Dirty

Billers receive many invitations to attend seminars on the fine art of diagnosis coding. The instructors are frequently medical records people who must be exact in their hospital reporting. They emphasize accuracy above all else. In the doctor's office, the diagnosis coding system was developed to collect information worldwide on the presence of disease. We must use the same system to defend charging for medical services. As an example, there are few patient problems not made worse by obesity. Since obesity is not the problem we are treating, it is not mentioned. In fact, many insurers may not pay for any service billed with the diagnosis of obesity.

Mental health and other programs may authorize a limited number of services and specify the diagnosis code to use for those visits. To be paid, you must report the authorized diagnosis even if the visit concerned other problems.

Also, the doctor's office may be limited to a few diagnoses per service. We simply must list first the "best" diagnosis code for the service. Diagnosis codes must be reasonable for the service performed. Always subject your coding to a reasonableness test. The next worksheet will show you how. The answers appear just before "Clinical Documentation Improvement (CDI) Impact on Coding: An Example." To ease the transition from ICD-9-CM to ICD-10-CM, minimal changes were made to both references in 2013.

Reasonableness Testing

Procedures and diagnoses must be reasonable; they must match each other. No one will declare it reasonable to x-ray a foot for a broken wrist. To assure that your choices come from the correct sections, the summary tables are presented below.

Diagnoses		Description
1.	A00–B99	Infectious/Parasitic Disease
2.	C00–D49	Neoplasms
3.	D50–D89	Blood/Blood-Forming/Immune
4.	E00–E89	Endocrine/Metabolic Diseases
5.	F01–F99	Mental/Behavior Disorders
6.	G00–G99	Nervous System
7.	H00–H59	Diseases Eye/Adnexa
8.	H60–H95	Diseases Ear/Mastoid
9.	I00–I99	Circulatory System
10.	J00–J99	Respiratory System
11.	K00–K99	Digestive System
12.	L00–L99	Skin/Subcutaneous Tissue
13.	M00–M99	Musculoskeletal/Connective Tissue
14.	N00–N99	Genitourinary System
15.	O00–O99	Pregnancy/Childbirth/Puerperium
16.	P00–P96	Conditions Perinatal Period
17.	Q00–Q99	Congenital Malformations
18.	R00–R99	Signs/Symptoms
19.	S00–T88	Injury/Poisoning/External causes
20.	V00–Y99	Morbidity Causes
21.	Z00–Z99	Health Status/Services

Procedures		Description
1.	99201–99499	Evaluation/Management
2.	00100–01999	Anesthesia
3.	10021–19499	Integumentary System
4.	20005–29999	Musculoskeletal System
5.	30000–32999	Respiratory System
6.	33010–37799	Cardiovascular System
7.	38100–39599	Hemic/Lymph/Mediastinum
8.	40490–49999	Digestive System
9.	50010–53899	Urinary System
10.	54000–55980	Male Genital/Intersex
11.	56405–59899	Female/Maternity
12.	60000–64999	Endocrine/Nervous Systems
13.	65091–68899	Eye/Ocular Adnexa
14.	69000–69990	Auditory System
15.	70010–79999	Radiology Services
16.	80047–89398	Pathology Services
17.	90281–99607	Medical Services
18.	0001F–0339T	Category II and III Codes

Using these tables, we can determine "reasonable" coding sections for procedures and diagnoses. If we assume there are no significant complications, we can select the reasonable code ranges for a fractured finger:

Diagnoses: Musculoskeletal (13), Injury (19)
Procedures: E/M (1), Musculoskeletal (4), Radiology (15)

Using the code section numbers, identify diagnoses and procedures for:

1. Headache: Diagnoses:
   Procedures:
2. Pneumothorax: Diagnoses:
   Procedures:
3. Ulcer: Diagnoses:
   Procedures:

Section IV. Diagnostic Coding and Reporting Guidelines for Outpatient Services

These coding guidelines for outpatient diagnoses have been approved for use by hospitals or providers in coding and reporting hospital-based outpatient services and provider-based office visits.

Information about the use of certain abbreviations, punctuation, symbols, and other conventions used in the ICD-10-CM Tabular List (code numbers and titles) can be found in Section IA of these guidelines, under "Conventions Used in the Tabular List." **Section IB contains general guidelines that apply to the entire classification. Section IC contains chapter-specific guidelines that correspond to the chapters as they are arranged in the classification.** Information about the correct sequence to use in finding a code is also described in Section I.

The terms *encounter* and *visit* are often used interchangeably in describing outpatient service contacts and, therefore, appear together in these guidelines without distinguishing one from the other.

Though the conventions and general guidelines apply to all settings, coding guidelines for outpatient and provider reporting of diagnoses will vary in a number of instances from those for inpatient diagnoses, recognizing that:

> The Uniform Hospital Discharge Data Set (UHDDS) definition of principal diagnosis applies only to inpatients in acute, short-term, long-term care and psychiatric hospitals.
>
> Coding guidelines for inconclusive diagnoses (probable, suspected, rule out, etc.) were developed for inpatient reporting and do not apply to outpatients.

A. Selection of first-listed condition

In the outpatient setting, the term first-listed diagnosis is used in lieu of principal diagnosis.

Adapted from ICD-10-CM Official Guidelines for Coding and Reporting.
Pages 103–107 of 117

In determining the first-listed diagnosis the coding conventions of ICD-10-CM, as well as the general and disease specific guidelines, take precedence over the outpatient guidelines.

Diagnoses often are not established at the time of the initial encounter or visit. It may take two or more visits before the diagnosis is confirmed.

The most critical rule involves beginning the search for the correct code assignment through the Alphabetic Index. Never begin searching initially in the Tabular List as this will lead to coding errors.

1. Outpatient Surgery

When a patient presents for outpatient surgery (same-day surgery), code the reason for the surgery as the first-listed diagnosis (reason for the encounter) even if the surgery is not performed due to a contraindication.

2. Observation Stay

When a patient is admitted for observation for a medical condition, assign a code for the medical condition as the first-listed diagnosis.

When a patient presents for outpatient surgery and develops complications requiring admission to observation, code the reason for the surgery as the first reported diagnosis (reason for the encounter) followed by codes for the complications as secondary diagnoses.

B. Codes from A00.0 through T88.9, Z00–Z99

The appropriate code(s) from A00.0 through T88.9, Z00–Z99 must be used to identify diagnoses, symptoms, conditions, problems, complaints, or other reason(s) for the encounter or visit.

C. Accurate reporting of ICD-10-CM diagnosis codes

For accurate reporting of ICD-10-CM diagnosis codes, the documentation should describe the patient's condition using terminology, which includes specific diagnoses as well as symptoms, problems, or reasons for the encounter. There are ICD-10-CM codes to describe all of these.

D. Codes that describe symptoms and signs

Codes that describe symptoms and signs, as opposed to diagnoses, are acceptable for reporting purposes when a diagnosis has not been established (confirmed) by the provider. Chapter 18 of ICD-10-CM, Symptoms, Signs, and Abnormal Clinical and Laboratory Findings Not Elsewhere Classified (codes R00–R99), contains many, but not all, codes for symptoms.

Adapted from ICD-10-CM Official Guidelines for Coding and Reporting.
Pages 103–107 of 117

E. Encounters for circumstances other than a disease or Injury

ICD-10-CM provides codes to deal with encounters for circumstances other than a disease or injury. The Factors Influencing Health Status and Contact with Health Services codes (Z00–Z99) are provided to deal with occasions when circumstances other than a disease or injury are recorded as diagnosis or problems.
See Section I.C.21. Factors Influencing Health Status and Contact with Health Services.

F. Level of detail in coding

1. ICD-10-CM codes with three, four, five, six, or seven characters

ICD-10-CM is composed of codes with three, four, five, six, or seven characters. Codes with three characters are included in ICD-10-CM as the heading of a category of codes that may be further subdivided by the use of fourth, fifth, sixth, or seventh characters to provide greater specificity.

2. Use of full number of characters required for a code

A three-character code is to be used only if it is not further subdivided. A code is invalid if it has not been coded to the full number of characters required for that code including the seventh character, if applicable.

G. ICD-10-CM code for the diagnosis, condition, problem, or other reason for encounter/visit

List first the ICD-10-CM code for the diagnosis, condition, problem, or other reason for encounter or visit shown in the medical record to be chiefly responsible for the services provided. List additional codes that describe any coexisting conditions. In some cases the first-listed diagnosis may be a symptom when a diagnosis has not been established (confirmed) by the physician.

H. Uncertain diagnosis

Do not code diagnoses documented as *probable*, *suspected*, *questionable*, *rule out*, or *working diagnosis* or other similar terms indicating uncertainty. Rather, code the condition(s) to the highest degree of certainty for that encounter or visit, such as symptoms, signs, abnormal test results, or other reason for the visit.

Please note: This differs from the coding practices used by short-term acute care, long-term care, and psychiatric hospitals.

I. Chronic diseases

Chronic diseases treated on an ongoing basis may be coded and reported as many times as the patient receives treatment and care for the condition(s).

Adapted from ICD-10-CM Official Guidelines for Coding and Reporting.
Pages 103–107 of 117

J. Code all documented conditions that coexist

Code all documented conditions that coexist at the time of the encounter or visit and that require or affect patient care treatment or management. Do not code conditions that were previously treated and no longer exist. However, history codes (categories Z80–Z87) may be used as secondary codes if the historical condition or family history has an impact on current care or influences treatment.

K. Patients receiving diagnostic services only

For patients receiving diagnostic services only during an encounter or visit, sequence first the diagnosis, condition, problem, or other reason for encounter or visit shown in the medical record to be chiefly responsible for the outpatient services provided during the encounter or visit. Codes for other diagnoses (e.g., chronic conditions) may be sequenced as additional diagnoses.

For encounters for routine laboratory or radiology testing, in the absence of any signs, symptoms, or associated diagnosis, assign Z01.89, encounter for other specified special examinations. If routine testing is performed during the same encounter as a test to evaluate a sign, symptom, or diagnosis, it is appropriate to assign both the Z code and the code describing the reason for the non-routine test.

For outpatient encounters for diagnostic tests that have been interpreted by a physician and for which the final report is available at the time of coding, code any confirmed or definitive diagnosis(es) documented in the interpretation. Do not code related signs and symptoms as additional diagnoses.

Please note: This differs from the coding practice in the hospital inpatient setting regarding abnormal findings on test results.

L. Patients receiving therapeutic services only

For patients receiving therapeutic services only during an encounter or visit, sequence first the diagnosis, condition, problem, or other reason for encounter or visit shown in the medical record to be chiefly responsible for the outpatient services provided during the encounter or visit. Codes for other diagnoses (e.g., chronic conditions) may be sequenced as additional diagnoses.

The only exception to this rule is that when the primary reason for the admission or encounter is chemotherapy or radiation therapy, the appropriate Z code for the service is listed first, and the diagnosis or problem for which the service is being performed listed second.

M. Patients receiving preoperative evaluations only

For patients receiving preoperative evaluations only, sequence first a code from subcategory Z01.81, encounter for pre-procedural examinations, to describe the pre-op consultations. Assign a code for the condition to describe the reason for the surgery as an additional diagnosis. Code also any findings related to the pre-op evaluation.

Adapted from ICD-10-CM Official Guidelines for Coding and Reporting.
Pages 103–107 of 117

N. Ambulatory surgery

For ambulatory surgery, code the diagnosis for which the surgery was performed. If the postoperative diagnosis is known to be different from the preoperative diagnosis at the time the diagnosis is confirmed, select the postoperative diagnosis for coding since it is the most definitive.

O. Routine outpatient prenatal visits

See Section I.C.15. Routine Outpatient Prenatal Visits.

P. Encounters for general medical examinations with abnormal findings

The subcategories for encounters of general medical examinations, Z00.0-, provide codes for with and without abnormal findings. Should a general medical examination result in an abnormal finding, the code for general medical examination with abnormal finding should be assigned as the first-listed diagnosis. A secondary code for the abnormal finding should also be coded.

Q. Encounters for routine health screenings

See Section I.C.21. Factors Influencing Health Status and Contact with Health Services, Screening.

Adapted from ICD-10-CM Official Guidelines for Coding and Reporting.
Pages 103–107 of 117
Courtesy of the Centers for Medicare & Medicaid Services, www.cms.hhs.gov

Moving from the old ICD-9-CM to the new ICD-10-CM

In the near future, health care providers using ICD-9-CM must begin reporting diagnoses from ICD-10-CM. This change in the coding process will amount to an expensive transition for providers, estimated at $99 million, $293 million, and $1.2 billion for small, medium, and large practices, respectively. But they are not alone. In September 2010, the Association for America's Health Insurance Plans (AHIP) estimated that costs of transition could reach $2 to $3 billion for insurers.

ICD-10-CM has over 69,000 codes; ICD-9-CM has fewer than 15,000 codes. ICD-10-CM has 21 chapters; ICD-9-CM has 19 chapters. ICD-10-CM codes are all alphanumeric; ICD-9-CM has only numeric codes except for the E and V codes. ICD-10-CM codes are three to seven characters in length; ICD-9-CM codes are three to five characters long.

If you presently code from ICD-9-CM for diagnoses and CPT for procedures, you will continue to use CPT with ICD-10-CM. If you currently code from ICD-9-CM Volume 3 (Procedures), you will use ICD-10-CM/PCS. ICD-10-PCS is replacing Volume 3 of ICD-9-CM and CMS is only requiring ICD-10-PCS for hospital inpatients. Because ICD-10-CM has not yet been printed in its final form, which is expected to become available in early in 2015, the following information comes from the 2014 draft publication of ICD-10-CM.

CMS announced a partial freeze on code changes prior to the implementation of ICD-10-CM. Code changes will be made only to capture new technology and new diseases.

ICD-10-CM has guidelines for reporting but the rules are more complex than the guidelines of ICD-9-CM. The coder will need a greater understanding of anatomy, physiology, and terminology to code correctly in ICD-10-CM. These guideline sections are as follows:

Section I: Conventions, general coding guidelines, and chapter-specific guidelines

Section II: Selection of principal diagnosis

Section III: Reporting additional diagnoses

Section IV: Diagnostic coding and reporting guidelines for outpatient services

Generally, Sections II and III are used for hospital reporting. Sections I and IV will be used most frequently by the physician's office coder.

Chapter-specific guidelines appear in Section I but have not yet been developed for the following:

D50–D89	Chapter 3: Diseases of Blood and Blood-forming Organs and Certain Disorders Involving the Immune Mechanism
H60–H95	Chapter 8: Diseases of the Ear and Mastoid Process
K00–K94	Chapter 11: Diseases of the Digestive System

There are significant notes at the start of each chapter in ICD-10-CM specifying how those codes are to be used. These instructions clarify many scenarios that have caused problems for coders over the years. While ICD-10-CM requires more precise coding, we are given additional directions for selecting the correct code.

Each chapter begins with information on what is included, what codes are never reported together (excludes 1), and the conditions that are not included in the code but may be reported with that code if both conditions exist (excludes 2). There's also a breakdown of the code blocks in that chapter, such as:

D00–D09	In situ neoplasms	P10–P15	Birth trauma	V00–X58	Accidents
K40–K46	Hernia	S80–S89	Injuries to the knee and lower leg	X92–Y08	Assault

The following table compares ICD-10-CM chapters with the chapters in ICD-9-CM:

ICD-10-CM Chapter/Name	Code Range
1. Certain Infectious and Parasitic Diseases	A00–B99
2. Neoplasms	C00–D49
3. Diseases of the Blood and Blood-forming Organs and Certain Disorders Involving the Immune Mechanism	D50–D89
4. Endocrine, Nutritional, and Metabolic Diseases	E00–E89
5. Mental and Behavioral Disorders	F01–F99
6. Diseases of the Nervous System	G00–G99
7. Diseases of the Eye and Adnexa	H00–H59
8. Diseases of the Ear and Mastoid Process	H60–H95
9. Diseases of the Circulatory System	I00–I99
10. Disease of the Respiratory System	J00–J99
11. Diseases of the Digestive System	K00–K94
12. Diseases of the Skin and Subcutaneous Tissue	L00–L99
13. Diseases of the Musculoskeletal System and Connective Tissue	M00–M99
14. Diseases of the Genitourinary System	N00–N99
15. Pregnancy, Childbirth, and the Puerperium	O00–O99
16. Certain Conditions Originating in the Perinatal Period	P00–P96
17. Congenital Malformations, Deformations, and Chromosomal Abnormalities	Q00–Q99
18. Symptoms, Signs, and Abnormal Clinical and Laboratory Findings, Not Elsewhere Classified	R00–R99
19. Injury, Poisoning, and Certain Other Consequences of External Causes	S00–T88
20. External Causes of Morbidity	V00–Y99
21. Factors Influencing Health Status and Contact with Health Services	Z00–Z99

ICD-9-CM Chapter/Name	Code Range
1. Infectious and Parasitic Diseases	001–139
2. Neoplasms	140–239
3. Endocrine, Nutritional, and Metabolic Diseases, and Immunity Disorders	240–279
4. Disease of Blood and Blood-forming Organs	280–289
5. Mental Disorders	290–319
6. Diseases of the Nervous System and Sense Organs	320–389
7. Diseases of the Circulatory System	390–459
8. Diseases of the Respiratory System	460–519
9. Diseases of the Digestive System	520–579
10. Diseases of the Genitourinary System	580–629
11. Complications of Pregnancy, Childbirth, and the Puerperium	630–679
12. Diseases of the Skin and Subcutaneous Tissue	680–709
13. Diseases of the Musculoskeletal System and Connective Tissue	710–739
14. Congenital Anomalies	740–759
15. Certain Conditions Originating in the Perinatal Period	760–779
16. Signs, Symptoms, and Ill-Defined Conditions	780–799
17. Injury and Poisoning	800–999
18. Classification of Factors Influencing Health Status and Contact with Health Service	V01–V91
19. Supplemental Classification of External Causes of Injury and Poisoning	E000–E999

ICD-10-CM codes are structured as follows:

Character	1	Alpha, except "U"
	2	Numeric
	3	Alpha or numeric (not case sensitive)
	4–7	Alpha or numeric (not case sensitive; may have an "x" as a place holder in positions 4–6)

ICD-10-CM uses all letters except "U" as the first character. The code will be invalid if the x's are omitted. All codes requiring a seventh character must include an x or xx unless the code is already six characters in length. The seventh character of the code gives specific information about the encounter or the medical condition. It must appear in the seventh position. The x is a placeholder to allow for the proper number of characters. The use of seventh characters are throughout the classification system. The majority of the seventh characters appear in Obstetrics and Injuries and Poisonings.

The seventh character may indicate that this is an initial encounter for this condition (A), that this is a subsequent encounter for fracture with delayed healing (G), or that this encounter is for the sequela of a condition (S). If this key information appears in any other position but the seventh, important data will be missing and therefore the code will be invalid. Code S82 ("fracture of the lower leg, including ankle") has 16 different letters for the seventh position. There are also notes stating that some of the 16 characters do not apply to certain subcategories of S82 (see "fracture of the patella," S82.0).

Since the place holder is not case sensitive, you may wish to use lower case for readability, as these are complex code configurations:

S61.022A	Initial encounter for a laceration with foreign body of left thumb without damage to nail
S77.02xA	Initial encounter for a crushing injury to the left hip
Y36.6x0S	Sequelae of war operations involving biological weapons encountered as a military personnel

Computer systems convert lower case letters to upper case for health care claims. If you haven't stopped using the lower case L for 1 (one) or continue to use the capital O for the number 0 (zero), get out of that habit now as this will create invalid codes when reporting in ICD-10-CM.

Organizations are introducing special references and online courses to provide a greater understanding of anatomy, physiology, and terminology described and used in ICD-10-CM. These may be especially helpful if you code from operative reports where the physician's terminology may not match the terms used in the coding system.

This material was prepared with the 2014 draft of ICD-10-CM. The final printed copy of ICD-10-CM may not be released before the implementation date, but CMS electronic files will have the most current edition.

ICD-10-CM has been described as a documentation problem rather than a coding issue. If the information is there, the coder can find the code. However, if the proper documentation is not in the medical record, coding becomes a guess, and an audit of the claim can follow. Since Medicare pays only for medically necessary services, your visits may be rejected if the same diagnosis code appears too often.

Coding Conflicts

It is not clear (yet) whether a claim will be rejected when a procedure code and modifiers do not match the new diagnosis coding structure. It is easy to see how this could occur.

Example 1:

Procedure:	Hallux valgus, right, Silver: 28290-T5
ICD-10-CM:	Hallux valgus (acquired), unspecified foot M20.11: Hallux valgus (acquired), right foot M20.12: Hallux valgus (acquired), left foot

Selecting a diagnosis code other than M20.11 will be incorrect. Will the claim be rejected with a mismatch between the procedure and diagnosis code? We simply don't know. The diagnosis code should correspond to the procedure code when reporting laterality.

Example 2:

Procedure:	Excise chalazion, right lower lid: 67800-RT or 67800-E4
ICD-10-CM:	H00.11: Chalazion, right upper eyelid H00.12: Chalazion, right lower eyelid H00.13: Chalazion, right eye, unspecified eyelid H00.14: Chalazion, left upper eyelid H00.15: Chalazion, left lower eyelid H00.16: Chalazion, left eye, unspecified eyelid H00.19: Chalazion, unspecified eye, unspecified eyelid

All these are incorrect diagnoses except H00.12. Let's hope our medical record documentation never results in having to select H00.19.

Will claims be rejected when we report a second initial encounter for the same condition reported last week? Will there be problems from reporting too many "unspecified" diagnoses? If we report an external cause code at subsequent encounters, will the claim reject?

At present, we do not know the answers to these questions. If we learn to code accurately in ICD-10-CM, we will never need to consider these possible problems.

Answers to the Reasonableness Test:

1.	Headache	Diagnosis: 5, 6, 9, 10, 13, 19	Procedure: 1, 4, 11, 12, 13, 15, 17
2.	Pneumothorax	Diagnosis: 10, 18, 19	Procedure: 1, 5, 15, 16, 17
3.	Ulcer	Gotcha! There isn't enough information here to code this one correctly. Is it a skin ulcer, mouth ulcer, or abdominal ulcer? Identify all the ulcer types you can think of, and code them all for diagnoses and procedures.	

Clinical Documentation Improvement (CDI) Impact on Coding: An Example

Since physician payments are based on the procedure code, the importance of the CPT code does not change with ICD-10-CM. However, diagnosis coding has not been critical in the past. We could use any reasonable code to allow payment. That is about to change. ICD-10-CM has codes based on laterality, severity, intent, and external causes. Payers will use this information to make certain they are paying claims appropriately. The addition of specific information in the medical record will allow coders to select the correct diagnosis code and hold off payer inquiries and avoid delayed payments.

Traditional documentation statement:

Mary Brown was treated for a painful small burn that she got this morning while making breakfast.

ICD-9-CM:	949.0—Burn, unspecified degree (there are 6.5 columns of burn codes) (ICD-9-CM note: "…extremely vague and should rarely be used."
ICD-10-CM:	T30.0—Burn of unspecified body region, unspecified degree (burn NOS) (Note: "Codes T20–T32 Burns and Corrosions are organized as burns by body site and degree.")
CPT:	99212 or 99213 or 16000—Initial treatment, first degree burn, when no more than local treatment is required

Better documentation statement:

Mary Brown was treated for a first degree painful small burn of the back of the left hand that she got this morning while making breakfast.

ICD-10-CM:	T23.162A—Burn of first degree of back of left hand (Note: Use additional code to identify the source, place, and intent of the burn.) (X00–X19, X75–X77, X96–X98, Y92). The external cause codes are not required by the federal government. State agencies and payers may require the external cause codes, but CMS does not require them for billing.

Correct documentation statement:

Mary Brown was treated for a painful small first degree burn at the back of the left hand that she got accidentally from the toaster this morning while making breakfast at home.

ICD-10-CM:	T23.162A	– and
	X15.1xxA	– initial visit, contact with a hot toaster, and
	Y92.010	– kitchen of a single family (private house) as the place of occurrence of the external cause.

Other occurrence possibilities:

Y92.020	Kitchen of a mobile home	Y92.030	Kitchen in an apartment
Y92.140	Kitchen in a prison	Y92.120	Kitchen in a nursing home
Y92.110	Kitchen in children's home and orphanage	Y92.22	Religious institution as place of occurrence of the external cause

A qualified medical assistant can record the body region, intent, and place of occurrence for the paper or electronic record. The provider determines the degree of burn and verifies the other information.

Certain Infectious and Parasitic Diseases (A00–B99)

The ICD-10-CM begins with **Chapter 1** on infectious and parasitic diseases. While many of these are not seen in the typical physician's office, they may be very significant in the offices of other doctors. Many of these conditions make headlines when they do occur. This chapter has specific guideline instructions for coding HIV, antibiotic resistance, sepsis, septic shock, SIRS, and MRSA. When coding HIV, use the B20 code for symptomatic confirmed cases; asymptomatic status is Z21. Move carefully through this chapter.

This chapter contains the following blocks:

A00–A09	Intestinal infectious diseases
A15–A19	Tuberculosis
A20–A28	Certain zoonotic bacterial diseases
A30–A49	Other bacterial diseases
A50–A64	Infections with a predominately sexual mode of transmission
A65–A69	Other spirochetal diseases
A70–A74	Other diseases caused by chlamydiae
A75–A79	Rickettsioses
A80–A89	Viral and infections of the central nervous system
A90–A99	Arthropod-borne viral fevers and viral hemorrhagic fevers
B10	Other human herpes viruses
B15–B19	Viral hepatitis
B20	Human immunodeficiency virus [HIV] disease
B25–B34	Other viral diseases
B35–B49	Mycoses
B50–B64	Protozoal diseases
B65–B83	Helminthiasis
B85–B89	Pediculosis, acariasis, and other infestations
B90–B94	Sequelae of infectious and parasitic diseases
B95–B97	Bacterial and viral infectious agents
B99	Other infectious diseases

ICD-10-CM contains extensive official guidelines on coding HIV/AIDS and sepsis. There are additional instructions in each subcategory of codes advising "code first" or "use additional code." Code only what is stated or known in the medical record. If no additional information is provided in the worksheet, code only the specific term(s).

Name ______________________

Using the blocks on the previous page as guidance, locate the three-character categories for the following diagnoses:

	Diagnoses	ICD-10-CM	ICD-9-CM
1.	Amebic abscess of brain, liver, and lungs		006.5
2.	Condyloma acuminatum		078.11
3.	Tuberculous mononeuropathy		
4.	Cytomegaloviral hepatitis		
5.	Head-louse infestation		
6.	Viral meningitis		047.9
7.	Swimmer's itch		120.3
8.	Chronic viral hepatitis		571.40
9.	Pinworm infection		127.40
10.	Bone and joint tuberculosis		

Name ______________________

Certain Infectious and Parasitic Diseases (A00–B99)

Using the alphabetic and tabular references, locate the following conditions and code to acceptable specificity, three to seven characters. Observe the coding instructions and include codes from other chapters as directed.

	Diagnoses	ICD-10-CM	ICD-9-CM
1.	Acute viral conjunctivitis from swimming pool	________	________
2.	Illness from bite of rabid dog	________	________
3.	Seven day fever	________	________
4.	Cranial neuritis from Lyme disease	________	________
5.	Ringworm	________	________
6.	Trichomonal fluor	________	________
7.	Syphilitic saddle nose	________	________
8.	Echovirus intestinal infection	________	________
9.	Dandy fever	________	________
10.	Ground itch	________	________
11.	Group A shigellosis	________	________
12.	Epstein-Barr viral mononucleosis with polyneuropathy	________	________
13.	Pseudocowpox	________	________
14.	Subacute spongiform encephalopathy with dementia	________	________
15.	Paratyphoid fever C	________	________
16.	Rubella encephalitis	________	________
17.	Australian X disease	________	________
18.	Pulmonary paracoccidioidomycosis	________	________
19.	Anaerobic sepsis	________	________
20.	AIDS related complex	________	________
21.	Early macular leprosy	________	________
22.	Lupus vulgaris tuberculosis	________	________
23.	Ebola viral fever	________	________
24.	African eyeworm	________	________
25.	Monkey malaria	________	________

Neoplasms (C00–D49)

Chapter 2 begins with notes on (a) functional activity, (b) morphology [histology], (c) primary malignant neoplasms overlapping site boundaries, and (d) malignant neoplasm of ectopic tissue. Read these notes carefully and observe these instructions when coding from this chapter. Note that malignant neoplasms begin with C while benign and in situ neoplasms begin with a D. Observe the chapter-specific guidelines for neoplasms and sequencing rules for coding surgical treatment of malignant tumors, radiation, and chemotherapy.

This chapter contains the following blocks:

C00–C14	Malignant neoplasm of lip, oral cavity, and pharynx
C15–C26	Malignant neoplasm of digestive organs
C30–C39	Malignant neoplasm of respiratory and intrathoracic organs
C40–C41	Malignant neoplasm of bone and articular cartilage
C43–C44	Melanoma and other malignant neoplasms of skin
C45–C49	Malignant neoplasms of mesothelial and soft tissue
C50	Malignant neoplasm of breast
C51–C58	Malignant neoplasms of female genital organs
C60–C63	Malignant neoplasms of male genital organs
C64–C68	Malignant neoplasm of the urinary tract
C69–C72	Malignant neoplasms of the eye, brain, and other parts of the central nervous system
C73–C75	Malignant neoplasms of thyroid and other endocrine glands
C7A	Malignant neuroendocrine tumors
C7B	Secondary neuroendocrine tumors
C76–C80	Malignant neoplasms of ill-defined, other secondary and unspecified sites
C81–C96	Malignant neoplasms of lymphoid, hematopoietic, and related tissue
D00–D09	In situ neoplasms
D10–D36	Benign neoplasms, except benign neuroendocrine tumors
D3A	Benign neuroendocrine tumors
D37–D48	Neoplasms of uncertain behavior, polycythemia vera, and myelodysplastic syndrome
D49	Neoplasms of unspecified behavior

There are additional instructions within each block of codes advising "excludes 1" or "use additional code." Code only what is stated or known in the medical record. If no additional information is provided in the worksheet, code only the specific term(s).

Name ______________________

Using the blocks on the previous page as guidance, locate the three-character categories for the following diagnoses:

	Diagnoses	ICD-10-CM	ICD-9-CM
1.	Malignant tumor of tongue border	________	141.2
2.	Benign heart neoplasm	________	212.7
3.	Carcinoma in site anal margin	________	232.5
4.	Acute myelomonocytic leukemia	________	________
5.	Malignant neoplasm of pancreas tail	________	________
6.	Kaposi's lung sarcoma	________	________
7.	Breast carcinoma in situ	________	________
8.	Benign frontal lobe tumor	________	________
9.	Malignancy of left lung, lower lobe	________	________
10.	Cancer of the bladder sphincter	________	________

Name ____________________

Neoplasms (C00–D49)

Using the alphabetic and tabular references, locate the following conditions and code to acceptable specificity, three to seven characters. Observe the coding instructions and include codes from other chapters as directed.

	Diagnoses	ICD-10-CM	ICD-9-CM
1.	Cardia carcinoma	________	________
2.	Primary cancer of the cauda equina	________	________
3.	Cancer of the lower lip vermillion border	________	________
4.	Adenoma of thalamus, thalamus	________	________
5.	Metastatic carcinoma to the brain tumor	________	________
6.	Dermatofibroma, left abdominal wall	________	________
7.	Occipital lobe brain cancer	________	________
8.	Metastasis to nabothian gland	________	________
9.	Tumor of Cowper's gland of Cowper's gland	________	________
10.	Benign growth, left eyebrow	________	________
11.	Metastatic lesion of the omentum	________	________
12.	Endometrial malignancy	________	________
13.	Benign neoplasm of the right renal pelvis	________	________
14.	Intramural uterine fibroid	________	________
15.	Cancer of the mesocolon	________	________
16.	Pancreatic duct cancer	________	________
17.	Benign lymphangioendothelioma	________	________
18.	Malignant neoplasm of right submaxillary gland	________	________
19.	In situ tracheal carcinoma	________	________
20.	Benign growth of the thymus	________	________
21.	Non-Hodgkins lymphoma, left axillary nodes	________	________
22.	Benign right breast tumor, 46-year-old male	________	________
23.	Cancer left lower lung lobe, 30+ years of tobacco use	________	________
24.	Retrobulbar malignancy, left eye	________	________
25.	Tonsil pillar carcinoma	________	________

Name ______________________

Diseases of the Blood and Blood-Forming Organs and Certain Disorders Involving the Immune Mechanism (D50–D89)

Chapter 3 begins with a note on the "excludes 2" in this chapter. Keep these exclusions in mind as you complete these worksheets. There are no chapter-specific coding guidelines for Chapter 3.

This chapter contains the following blocks:

D50–D53	Nutritional anemias
D55–D59	Hemolytic anemias
D60–D64	Aplastic and other anemias and other bone marrow failure syndromes
D65–D69	Coagulation defects, purpura, and other hemorrhagic conditions
D70–D77	Other disorders of blood and blood-forming organs
D78	Intraoperative and post procedural complication of the spleen
D80–D89	Certain disorders involving the immune mechanism

There are additional instructions within each block of codes advising "includes," "excludes 1," or "use additional code." Code only what is stated or known in the medical record. If no additional information is provided in the worksheet, code only the specific term(s).

Using the above blocks as guidance, locate the three-character categories for the following diagnoses:

	Diagnoses	ICD-10-CM	ICD-9-CM
1.	Christmas disease	______	286.1
2.	Cooley's anemia	______	282.44
3.	Infantile pseudoleukemia	______	285.8
4.	March hemoglobinuria	______	______
5.	Imerslund syndrome	______	______
6.	Aplastic anemia, NOS	______	______
7.	Hereditary leukomelanopathy	______	______
8.	Sideropenic dysphagia	______	______
9.	Emotional polycythemia	______	______
10.	Megakaryocytic hypoplasia	______	______

Name ______________________

Diseases of the Blood and Blood-Forming Organs and Certain Disorders Involving the Immune Mechanism (D50–D89)

Using the alphabetic and tabular references, locate the following conditions and code to acceptable specificity, three to seven characters. Observe the coding instructions and include codes from other chapters as directed.

	Diagnoses	ICD-10-CM	ICD-9-CM
1.	Antithromboplastinemia	________	________
2.	Paroxysmal cold disease	________	________
3.	Thrombocytopenia from extracorporeal blood circulation	________	________
4.	Hypergammaglobulinemia	________	________
5.	Megaloblastic anemia	________	________
6.	Siderotic splenomegaly	________	________
7.	Chronic hemoglobin Hb-SS disease	________	________
8.	Plummer-Vinson syndrome	________	________
9.	Antineoplastic chemotherapy induced pancytopenia	________	________
10.	Iron deficiency anemia	________	________
11.	Mechanical hemolytic anemia	________	________
12.	Vegan anemia	________	________
13.	Von Willebrand's disease	________	________
14.	Lazy leukocyte syndrome	________	________
15.	Classical hemophilia	________	________
16.	Intraoperative hemorrhage of spleen during surgery on the spleen	________	________
17.	Splenitis	________	________
18.	Stomatocytosis	________	________
19.	Ideopathic allergic eosinophilia	________	________
20.	Thrombocytopathy	________	________
21.	Thalassemic variants	________	________
22.	Blackfan-Diamond syndrome	________	________
23.	Lymphocytopenia	________	________
24.	Consumption coagulopathy	________	________
25.	Goat's milk anemia	________	________

Name ____________________

Endocrine, Nutritional, and Metabolic Diseases (E00–E89)

Chapter 4 begins with notes stating all neoplasms are classified in Chapter 2; and codes E05.8, E07.0, E16–E31 and E34– may be used as additional codes. Also there is a general exclusion for transitory endocrine and metabolic disorders in a newborn. This chapter is where you find codes for Type 1 and Type 2 diabetes, thyroid problems, and obesity. Note that obesity is defined as a BMI of 30.0 and above. Be certain you review carefully the chapter-specific coding guidelines for Chapter 4.

This chapter contains the following blocks:

E00–E07	Disorders of thyroid gland
E08–E13	Diabetes mellitus
E15–E16	Other disorders of glucose regulation and pancreatic internal secretion
E20–E35	Disorders of other endocrine glands
E36	Intraoperative complications of endocrine system
E40–E46	Malnutrition
E50–E64	Other nutritional deficiencies
E65–E68	Overweight, obesity, and other hyperalimentation
E70–E88	Metabolic disorders
E89	Postprocedural endocrine and metabolic complications and disorders, not elsewhere classified

There are additional instructions within each block of codes advising "includes," "excludes 1," "excludes 2," "code also," or "use additional code." Code only what is stated or known in the medical record. If no additional information is provided in the worksheet, code only the specific term(s). Note that intraoperative and postprocedural complications appear in separate blocks and are separately coded in this chapter.

Using the above blocks as guidance, locate the three-character categories for the following diagnoses:

	Diagnoses	ICD-10-CM	ICD-9-CM
1.	Type I diabetes	________	250.1
2.	Stein-Leventhal syndrome	________	256.4
3.	Simple nontoxic goiter	________	241.9
4.	Maple-syrup-urine disease	________	________
5.	Dysmetabolic syndrome X	________	________
6.	Familial hypercholesterolemia	________	________
7.	Postpancreatectomy diabetes mellitus	________	________
8.	Excess calorie morbid obesity	________	________
9.	Wermer's syndrome	________	________
10.	Hypoglycemia	________	________

Name ____________________

Endocrine, Nutritional, and Metabolic Diseases (E00–E89)

Using the alphabetic and tabular references, locate the following conditions and code to acceptable specificity, three to seven characters. Observe the coding instructions and include codes from other chapters as directed.

	Diagnoses	ICD-10-CM	ICD-9-CM
1.	Hashimoto's disease	____	____
2.	Pseudohypoparathyroidism	____	____
3.	Type 1 diabetes with diabetic cataract	____	____
4.	Adrenal crisis	____	____
5.	Night blindness from vitamin A deficiency	____	____
6.	Graves' disease with thyrotoxic storm	____	____
7.	Type 2 diabetes with Charcot's joints	____	____
8.	Symptoms of early menopause	____	____
9.	Group B hyperlipidemia	____	____
10.	Diabetes from Cushing's syndrome	____	____
11.	Elevated cholesterol and triglycerides	____	____
12.	Well-controlled long-term insulin dependence diabetes, Type 2	____	____
13.	Lactose intolerant	____	____
14.	Brittle Type I diabetes with mild chronic kidney disease	____	____
15.	Marasmic kwashiorkor	____	____
16.	Diabetes insipidus	____	____
17.	Type I diabetes, small superficial skin ulcer, left heel and midfoot	____	____
18.	de Quervain syndrome	____	____
19.	Bowlegs from rickets, now inactive	____	____
20.	Fertile eunuch syndrome	____	____
21.	X-linked adrenoleukodystrophy, age 15	____	____
22.	Pickwickian syndrome	____	____
23.	Pulmonary cystic fibrosis	____	____
24.	Type 2 diabetes, nonproliferative retinopathy and macular edema	____	____
25.	Hemorrhage/hematoma of thyroid during neck CA surgery	____	____

Name ______________________

Mental, Behavioral, and Neurodevelopmental Disorders (F01–F99)

Chapter 5 advises that psychological development disorders are included in this chapter. The "excludes 2" instruction notes that symptoms, signs and abnormal clinical laboratory findings, not elsewhere classified, are R00–R99. There are codes here for use, abuse, and dependence on substances; schizophrenia, depression, bipolar I and II, anorexia, gambling, ADHD, and intellectual disabilities, sometimes called mental retardation, are included in this chapter. There are chapter-specific coding guidelines for pain and disorders due to psychoactive substance use.

This chapter contains the following blocks:

F01–F09	Mental disorders due to known physiological conditions
F10–F19	Mental and behavioral disorders due to psychoactive substance use
F20–F29	Schizophrenia, schizotypal, delusional, and other non-mood psychotic disorders
F30–F39	Mood [affective] disorders
F40–F48	Anxiety, dissociative, stress-related, somatoform, and other nonpsychotic mental disorders
F50–F59	Behavioral syndromes associated with physiological disturbances and physical factors
F60–F69	Disorders of adult personality and behavior
F70–F79	Intellectual disabilities
F80–F89	Pervasive and specific developmental disorders
F90–F98	Behavioral and emotional disorders with onset usually occurring in childhood and adolescence
F99	Unspecified mental disorder

There are additional instructions within each block of codes advising "includes," "excludes 1," "excludes 2," "code first," or "use additional code." Code only what is stated or known in the medical record. If no additional information is provided in the worksheet, code only the specific term(s).

Using the above blocks as guidance, locate the three-character categories for the following diagnoses:

	Diagnoses	ICD-10-CM	ICD-9-CM
1.	Nail-biting	________	307.9
2.	Aggressive personality disorder	________	301.3
3.	Depressive neurosis	________	300.4
4.	Intoxication from marijuana dependence	________	________
5.	Paranoia	________	________
6.	Dementia with combative behavior	________	________
7.	Frontal lobe syndrome	________	________
8.	Post-traumatic stress disorder	________	________
9.	Delirium from alcohol withdrawal	________	________
10.	Kleptomania	________	________

Name ____________________

Mental, Behavioral, and Neurodevelopmental Disorders (F01–F99)

Using the alphabetic and tabular references, locate the following conditions and code to acceptable specificity, three to seven characters. Observe the coding instructions and include codes from other chapters as directed.

	Diagnoses	ICD-10-CM	ICD-9-CM
1.	Simple opioid dependence	________	________
2.	Weekend glue sniffing abuse	________	________
3.	Obsessive-compulsive personality	________	________
4.	Frequent panic attacks	________	________
5.	Asperger's disorder since age 4	________	________
6.	Intoxication delirium from cannabis abuse	________	________
7.	Post partum depression	________	________
8.	Dysthymic personality disorder	________	________
9.	Alcoholic acute drunkenness	________	________
10.	Acute infective psychosis	________	________
11.	Exhibitionism	________	________
12.	Undifferentiated chronic schizophrenia	________	________
13.	Excessive fear of injections	________	________
14.	IQ 27	________	________
15.	PCP abuse with intoxication with perceptual disturbance	________	________
16.	Stuttering, four-year-old male	________	________
17.	Hyperactive and inattentive attention-deficit disorder	________	________
18.	Borderline schizophrenic	________	________
19.	Childhood social anxiety	________	________
20.	Anorexia nervosa	________	________
21.	Adjustment reaction anxiety and depression	________	________
22.	Bipolar, current episode manic without psychosis	________	________
23.	Multiple personality disorder	________	________
24.	Childhood pica disorder	________	________
25.	Four-year-old girl with reactive attachment disorder	________	________

Name ______________________

Diseases of the Nervous System (G00–G99)

Chapter 6 begins with a list of "excludes 2" conditions that appear in other chapters. Observe these and other instructions for coding epilepsy (seizure disorders) and sequencing headaches and other pain symptoms. The chapter-specific coding guidelines provide instruction on dominant or nondominant side and the use of the pain codes in this chapter.

This chapter contains the following blocks:

G00–G09	Inflammatory diseases of the central nervous system
G10–G14	Systemic atrophies primarily affecting the central nervous system
G20–G26	Extrapyramidal and movement disorders
G30–G32	Other degenerative diseases of the nervous system
G35–G37	Demyelinating diseases of the central nervous system
G40–G47	Episodic and paroxysmal disorders
G50–G59	Nerve, nerve root and plexus disorders
G60–G65	Polyneuropathies and other disorders of the peripheral nervous system
G70–G73	Diseases of myoneural junction and muscle
G80–G83	Cerebral palsy and other paralytic syndromes
G89–G99	Other disorders of the nervous system

There are additional instructions within each block of codes advising "excludes 1," "excludes 2," "code first," "code also," or "use additional code." Code only what is stated or known in the medical record. If no additional information is provided in the worksheet, code only the specific term(s).

Using the above blocks as guidance, locate the three-character categories for the following diagnoses:

Diagnoses	ICD-10-CM	ICD-9-CM
1. Pneumococcal meningitis	________	________
2. Communicating hydrocephalus	________	________
3. ALS	________	________
4. Periodic paralysis	________	________
5. Ideopathic nasal leak of cerebrospinal fluid	________	________
6. Necrotizing hemorrhagic encephalopathy, acute	________	________
7. Right carpal tunnel	________	________
8. Menstrual related hypersomnia	________	________
9. Parkinsonism	________	________
10. Guillian-Barre syndrome	________	________

Name ____________________

Diseases of the Nervous System (G00–G99)

Using the alphabetic and tabular references, locate the following conditions and code to acceptable specificity, three to seven characters. Observe the coding instructions and include codes from other chapters as directed.

	Diagnoses	ICD-10-CM	ICD-9-CM
1.	Tarsal tunnel syndrome, right		
2.	Huntington's chorea		
3.	Accidental lumbar puncture with fluid leak		
4.	Premenstrual tension syndrome with intractable migraine		
5.	Dementia with Lewy bodies		
6.	Hereditary Friedreich's ataxia		
7.	Narcolepsy and cataplexy, 15-year-old male		
8.	Tic douloureux		
9.	Pyogenic meningitis		
10.	Bilateral long-term upper diplegia		
11.	Acute motor neuropathy		
12.	Stiff-man syndrome		
13.	Neurogenic bladder from cauda equina		
14.	Duchenne muscular dystrophy		
15.	Early onset Alzheimer's		
16.	Multiple sclerosis		
17.	Myopathy from methanol overdose last year		
18.	Torticollis, spasmodic type		
19.	Inflammatory demyelinating polyneuropathy, chronic		
20.	Chronic migraine, no aura		
21.	Meningitis, chronic		
22.	Reye's syndrome		
23.	Werdnig-Hoffman disease		
24.	Painful phantom limb syndrome		
25.	Chronic tension-type headache		

Name ____________________

Diseases of the Eye and Adnexa (H00–H59)

Chapter 7 begins with a note to use an external cause code following the code for the eye condition, if applicable, to identify the cause of the eye condition. This is basically a "code also" instruction. Review carefully the extensive list of "excludes 2" conditions that may be the cause of the eye condition. Many of these are repeated in the individual blocks of codes. Note also that the glaucoma subcategory contains the first regular use of the "X" as a place holder to put the seventh character in the proper position. The chapter-specific guidelines provide direction on the use of the glaucoma codes.

This chapter contains the following blocks:

H00–H05	Disorders of the eyelid, lacrimal system, and orbit
H10–H11	Disorders of conjunctiva
H15–H22	Disorders of sclera, cornea, iris, and ciliary body
H25–H28	Disorders of lens
H30–H36	Disorders of choroid and retina
H40–H42	Glaucoma
H43–H44	Disorders of vitreous body and globe
H46–H47	Disorders of optic nerve and visual pathways
H49–H52	Disorders of ocular muscles, binocular movement, accommodation, and refraction
H53–H54	Visual disturbances and blindness
H55–H57	Other disorders of eye and adnexa
H59	Intraoperative and postprocedureal complications and disorders of eye and adnexa, not elsewhere classified

There are additional instructions within each block of codes advising "excludes 1," "excludes 2," "code first," "code also," or "use additional code." Code only what is stated or known in the medical record. If no additional information is provided in the worksheet, code only the specific term(s).

Using the above blocks as guidance, locate the three-character categories for the following diagnoses:

	Diagnoses	ICD-10-CM	ICD-9-CM
1.	Senile ectropion, right lower lid	________	________
2.	Poor drainage, right epiphora	________	________
3.	Abscess, right cornea	________	________
4.	Vitreous floaters	________	________
5.	Left age-related posterior subcapsular cataract	________	________
6.	Hemorrhage, right conjunctiva	________	________
7.	Left total retinal detachment	________	________
8.	Old-age macular degeneration	________	________
9.	Presbyopia	________	________
10.	Bilateral chronic conjunctivitis, uncomplicated	________	________

Name ______________________

Diseases of the Eye and Adnexa (H00–H59)

Using the alphabetic and tabular references, locate the following conditions and code to acceptable specificity, three to seven characters. Observe the coding instructions and include codes from other chapters as directed. Watch for the abbreviations FB (foreign body), OD (right eye), OS (left eye), and OU (both eyes).

	Diagnoses	ICD-10-CM	ICD-9-CM
1.	Bilateral irregular astigmatism	________	367.22
2.	Stye, left lower lid	________	373.11
3.	Prematurity retinopathy, stage 1, OU	________	________
4.	Juvenile nuclear cataract, OS	________	________
5.	Dermatitis (eczema) of left upper lid	________	________
6.	Conjunctival pseudopterygium, OD	________	________
7.	Moderate low-tension glaucoma, OS	________	________
8.	Keratoconus, acute hydrops, OD	________	________
9.	Pupillary margin degeneration, OS	________	________
10.	Retinitis pigmentosa	________	________
11.	Old metal FB, right lower lid	________	________
12.	Scotoma, blindspot, OS	________	________
13.	Bilateral retinopathy from the sun	________	________
14.	Dry eye syndrome, OU	________	________
15.	Open angle glaucoma, high risk, OS	________	________
16.	Chronic allergic conjunctivitis, OU	________	________
17.	Snow blindness, OU	________	________
18.	Aphakia	________	________
19.	Retained FB (nail head), right anterior chamber	________	________
20.	Old-age nuclear cataracts, OU	________	________
21.	Right central vein occlusion	________	________
22.	Color-blind	________	________
23.	Dissociated nystagmus	________	________
24.	Convergent strabismus, alternating A pattern	________	________
25.	Left chorioretinal scarring from old retinal detachment surgery	________	________

Name ____________________

Diseases of the Ear and Mastoid Process (H60–H95)

Chapter 8 begins with a note to use the external cause code, if applicable, after the code for the ear condition to identify the cause of the ear condition. Review the "excludes 2" list on conditions that are coded in other chapters. There are no chapter-specific coding guidelines for Chapter 8.

This chapter contains the following blocks:

H60–H62	Diseases of the external ear
H65–H75	Diseases of the middle ear and mastoid
H80–H63	Diseases of the inner ear
H90–H94	Other disorders of the ear
H95	Intraoperative and postprocedural complications and disorders of the ear and mastoid process, not elsewhere classified

There are additional instructions within each block of codes advising "includes," "excludes 1," "excludes 2," "code first," or "use additional code." Code only what is stated or known in the medical record. If no additional information is provided in the worksheet, code only the specific term(s).

Using the above blocks as guidance, locate the three-character categories for the following diagnoses:

	Diagnoses	ICD-10-CM	ICD-9-CM
1.	Right attic cholesteatoma	________	385.31
2.	Boil, left external ear	________	680.0
3.	Bilateral Meniere's disease	________	386.61
4.	Otitis media, right	________	382.9
5.	Left chronic myringitis	________	384.1
6.	Left pinna perichondritis	________	________
7.	Bilateral presbycusis	________	________
8.	Tinnitus, right	________	________
9.	Mixed left hearing loss, normal right hearing	________	________
10.	Chronic mastoiditis	________	________

Name ______________________

Diseases of the Ear and Mastoid Process (H60–H95)

Using the alphabetic and tabular references, locate the following conditions and code to acceptable specificity, three to seven characters. Observe the coding instructions and include codes from other chapters as directed.

	Diagnoses	ICD-10-CM	ICD-9-CM
1.	Otalgia, right ear		
2.	Bilateral swimmer's ear		
3.	Sudden left idiopathic hearing loss		
4.	Bilateral sensorineural hearing loss		
5.	Right labyrinthine fistula		
6.	Bilateral chronic mastoiditis		
7.	Four marginal tympanic membrane perforations, left		
8.	Left acoustic nerve disorder		
9.	Central positional nystagmus, left		
10.	Right bullous myringitis		
11.	Bony obstruction, right Eustachian tube		
12.	Right round window otosclerosis		
13.	Recurrent cholesteatoma in left mastoidectomy cavity		
14.	Otitis externa with hemorrhage, left		
15.	Bilateral hearing loss from loud music		
16.	Glue in left ear		
17.	Bilateral impacted cerumen		
18.	Right petrous bone inflammation		
19.	Labyrinthitis, left ear		
20.	Bilateral high frequency hearing loss		
21.	Right mastoid cholesteatoma		
22.	Total perforation, left tympanic membrane		
23.	Right middle ear polyp		
24.	Severe left Meniere's disease		
25.	Six-year-old with chronic bilateral serous otitis media, both parents are smokers		

Name ______________________

Diseases of the Circulatory System (I00–I99)

Review the extensive "excludes 2" list on conditions that are coded in other chapters. **Chapter 9** codes will be used in many medical offices and some forms of the words can be confusing. Note that these codes begin with an "I," not the number "1." Move slowly through this chapter. Atherosclerosis is defined as the plaque buildup that occurs inside blood vessels. This chapter includes codes for hypertension, hypertensive heart disease with chronic kidney disease, angina, myocardial infarction (heart attack), and cerebrovascular disease. Specific chapter guidelines provide instruction on coding coronary heart disease (also called coronary artery disease) and other coronary and cerebrovascular conditions.

This chapter contains the following blocks:

I00–I02	Acute rheumatic fever
I05–I09	Chronic rheumatic heart diseases
I10–I15	Hypertensive diseases
I20–I25	Ischemic heart disease
I26–I28	Pulmonary heart disease and diseases of pulmonary circulation
I30–I15	Other forms of heart disease
I60–I69	Cerebrovascular diseases
I70–I79	Diseases of arteries, arterioles, and capillaries
I80–I89	Diseases of veins, lymphatic vessels, and lymph nodes, not elsewhere classified
I95–I99	Other and unspecified disorders of the circulatory system

There are additional instructions within each block of codes advising "includes," "excludes 1," "excludes 2," "code first," "code also," or "use additional code." Code only what is stated or known in the medical record. If no additional information is provided in the worksheet, code only the specific term(s).

Using the above blocks as guidance, locate the three-character categories for the following diagnoses:

Diagnoses	ICD-10-CM	ICD-9-CM
1. Postural hypotension	______	458.0
2. Buerger's disease	______	443.1
3. Acute diastolic heart disease	______	429.9
4. Chronic ischemic heart disease	______	______
5. Rheumatic mitral regurgitation	______	396.3
6. Mobitz II block	______	______
7. Left lower leg varicose veins with toe ulcer	______	______
8. High blood pressure	______	______
9. Subacute endocarditis	______	______
10. Unruptured cerebral aneurysm	______	______

Name ______________________

Diseases of the Circulatory System (I00–I99)

Using the alphabetic and tabular references, locate the following conditions and code to acceptable specificity, three to seven characters. Observe the coding instructions and include codes from other chapters as directed.

	Diagnoses	ICD-10-CM	ICD-9-CM
1.	Mitral valve insufficiency with aortic valve stenosis	________	396.2
2.	Sick sinus syndrome	________	427.81
3.	Hypertensive heart disease	________	________
4.	Dysphasia from cerebrovascular disease	________	________
5.	Unstable angina	________	________
6.	Left ankle ulcer from leg atherosclerosis	________	________
7.	Thrombosis of left vertebral artery with infarction	________	________
8.	Congestive heart failure	________	________
9.	Healed myocardial infarction	________	________
10.	Left vertebral artery stenosis and occlusion	________	________
11.	Unruptured abdominal aortic aneurysm	________	________
12.	Variocele	________	________
13.	Postmastectomy elephantiasis	________	________
14.	Bypass graft atherosclerosis with unstable angina	________	________
15.	Thrombophlebitis and phlebitis, left femoral vein	________	________
16.	Bilateral varicose leg veins, asymptomatic	________	________
17.	Alcohol dependence with alcoholic cardiomyopathy	________	________
18.	Cardiorenal hypertension, stage 2 kidney disease	________	________
19.	Intermittent claudication	________	________
20.	Idiopathic gangrene	________	________
21.	STEMI of left anterior descending coronary artery	________	________
22.	Varicose veins, both legs with extensive swelling	________	________
23.	Raynaud's disease	________	________
24.	Pulmonary hypertension	________	________
25.	Chronic atrial fibrillation	________	________

Name ____________________

Diseases of the Respiratory System (J00–J99)

Chapter 10 begins with a note: When a respiratory condition is described as occurring in more than one site and is not specifically indexed, it should be classified to the lower anatomic site (e.g. tracheobronchitis to bronchitis in J40). The terms acute, chronic, and acute exacerbation of a chronic disorder, and other conditions could change the coding order. Observe the chapter-specific coding guidelines for COPD, asthma, influenza, and pneumonia.

This chapter contains the following blocks:

J00–J06	Acute upper respiratory infections
J09–J18	Influenza and pneumonia
J20–J22	Other acute lower respiratory infections
J30–J39	Other diseases of the upper respiratory tract
J40–J47	Chronic lower respiratory diseases
J60–J70	Lung diseases due to external agents
J80–J84	Other respiratory diseases principally affecting the interstitium
J85–J86	Suppurative and necrotic conditions of the lower respiratory tract
J90–J94	Other diseases of the pleura
J95	Intraoperative and postprocedural complications and disorders of respiratory system, not elsewhere classified
J96–J99	Other diseases of the respiratory system

There are additional instructions within each block of codes advising "includes," "excludes 1," "excludes 2," "code first," "code also," or "use additional code." Code only what is stated or known in the medical record. If no additional information is provided in the worksheet, code only the specific term(s).

Using the above blocks as guidance, locate the three-character categories for the following diagnoses:

	Diagnoses	ICD-10-CM	ICD-9-CM
1.	Pulmonary edema	________	514.
2.	Mild intermittent asthma	________	493.96
3.	Common cold	________	460.
4.	Mendelson's syndrome	________	997.32
5.	Acute chemical bronchitis	________	506.0
6.	Influenza	________	________
7.	Quinsy	________	________
8.	Black lung disease	________	________
9.	Acute rhinovirus bronchitis	________	________
10.	Severe acute respiratory syndrome	________	________

Name ______________________

Diseases of the Respiratory System (J00–J99)

Using the alphabetic and tabular references, locate the following conditions and code to acceptable specificity, three to seven characters. Observe the coding instructions and include codes from other chapters as directed.

	Diagnoses	ICD-10-CM	ICD-9-CM
1.	Pollen induced allergic rhinitis		477.0
2.	Acute sinus infection		461.9
3.	Chronic tonsillitis, currently 40+ years of tobacco dependence		
4.	Mediastinal emphysema		
5.	Laryngeal edema		
6.	Silicosis		
7.	A/H5N1 Influenza with pneumonia		
8.	Asthma with status asthamaticus		
9.	Pulmonary fibrosis, idiopathic		
10.	Return visit for lung fibrosis from radon exposure		
11.	Chronic bronchitis		
12.	*E. coli* bronchopneumonia		
13.	Hypoxia with chronic respiratory failure		
14.	COPD		
15.	Spontaneous pneumothorax due to Marfan's syndrome		
16.	Pulmonary interstitial glycogenosis, 4-day-old infant		
17.	Respiratory trouble from smoke inhalation		
18.	Frontal sinus infection		
19.	Aspiration pneumonia		
20.	Pleural effusion		
21.	Laryngotracheitis		
22.	Right maxillary sinus polyp		
23.	Methacillin resistant *Staphylococcus aureus* pneumonia		
24.	Acute bronchiolitis		
25.	Pulmonary emphysema		

Name ____________________

Diseases of the Digestive System (K00–K95)

There are no chapter-specific coding guidelines for **Chapter 11**. There is an extensive list of "excludes 2" conditions that appear in other chapters. Review and observe these exclusions when coding digestive disorders including hernias and noninfective enteritis and colitis, including Crohn's disease.

This chapter contains the following blocks:

K00–K14	Diseases of oral cavity and salivary glands
K20–K31	Diseases of esophagus, stomach, and duodenum
K35–K39	Diseases of appendix
K40–K46	Hernia
K50–K52	Noninfective enteritis and colitis
K55–K64	Other diseases of intestines
K65–K68	Diseases of peritoneum and retroperitoneum
K70–K77	Diseases of liver
K80–K87	Disorders of gallbladder, biliary tract, and pancreas
K90–K95	Other diseases of the digestive system

There are additional instructions within each block of codes advising "includes," "excludes 1," "excludes 2," "code first," "use additional code," or "code also." Code only what is stated or known in the medical record. If no additional information is provided in the worksheet, code only the specific term(s).

Using the above blocks as guidance, locate the three-character categories for the following diagnoses:

Diagnoses	ICD-10-CM	ICD-9-CM
1. Right inguinal hernia	____________	553.9
2. Mesenteric lipodystrophy	____________	567.82
3. Cirrhosis of the liver	____________	571.5
4. Microdontia	____________	520.2
5. Gastric band infection	____________	535.50
6. Acute appendicitis	____________	____________
7. Regional colitis	____________	____________
8. Hemorrhagic angiodysplasia of the colon	____________	____________
9. Gallbladder gangrene	____________	____________
10. Esophageal erosion	____________	____________

Name ____________________

Diseases of the Digestive System (K00–K95)

Using the alphabetic and tabular references, locate the following conditions and code to acceptable specificity, three to seven characters. Observe the coding instructions and include codes from other chapters as directed.

	Diagnoses	ICD-10-CM	ICD-9-CM
1.	Stricture and stenosis of salivary duct, left	________	________
2.	Ruptured appendix with peritonitis	________	________
3.	Irritable bowel syndrome	________	________
4.	Chronic hemorrhage from a gastric ulcer	________	________
5.	Impacted left lower wisdom tooth	________	________
6.	Crohn's disease with fistula	________	________
7.	Strangulated midline ventral hernia	________	________
8.	Chronic gastritis	________	________
9.	Perianal abscess	________	________
10.	Nonalcoholic fatty liver disease	________	________
11.	Significant aphthous stomatitis	________	________
12.	Celiac disease	________	________
13.	Post-op dumping syndrome	________	________
14.	Chronic appendicitis	________	________
15.	Liver problems caused by schistosomiasis	________	________
16.	Sialoadenitis, acute	________	________
17.	Chronic cholecystis with obstruction and bile duct stone	________	________
18.	Post-op pelvic adhesions, 46-year-old male	________	________
19.	Chronic duodenal ulcer	________	________
20.	Diverticulosis of large and small intestine	________	________
21.	Colon polyp	________	________
22.	Obstructed incarcerated umbilical hernia	________	________
23.	Chronic gingivitis from plaque	________	________
24.	Acute pancreatitis due to alcohol abuse	________	________
25.	Recurrent gastroenteritis and colitis following suicide attempt (methanol) 12 years ago	________	________

Name ______________________

Diseases of the Skin and Subcutaneous Tissue (L00–L99)

Chapter 12 begins with an extensive list of "excludes 2" conditions that appear in other chapters. There are chapter-specific coding guidelines for documenting and coding the staging of pressure ulcers.

This chapter contains the following blocks:

L00–L08	Infections of the skin and subcutaneous tissue
L10–L14	Bullous disorders
L20–L30	Dermatitis and eczema
L40–L45	Papulosquamous disorders
L49–L54	Urticaria and erythema
L55–L59	Radiation-related disorders of the skin and subcutaneous tissue
L6O–L75	Disorders of skin appendages
L76	Intraoperative and postprocedural complications of skin and subcutaneous tissue
L80–L99	Other disorders of the skin and subcutaneous tissue

There are additional instructions within each block of codes advising "includes," "excludes 1," "excludes 2," "code first," "use additional code," or "code also." Code only what is stated or known in the medical record. If no additional information is provided in the worksheet, code only the specific term(s).

Using the above blocks as guidance, locate the three-character categories for the following diagnoses:

	Diagnoses	ICD-10-CM	ICD-9-CM
1.	Duhring's disease	________	________
2.	Psoriatic arthritis mutilans	________	________
3.	Boil on the left scapula	________	________
4.	Nonbullous erythema multiformae	________	________
5.	Hyperhydrosis	________	________
6.	Allergic dermatitis from face cream	________	________
7.	Cradle cap	________	________
8.	Corn on left great toe	________	________
9.	Pilonidal abscess	________	________
10.	Senile keratosis	________	________

2-W.

Name ______________________

Diseases of the Skin and Subcutaneous Tissue (L00–L99)

Using the alphabetic and tabular references, locate the following conditions and code to acceptable specificity, three to seven characters. Observe the coding instructions and include codes from other chapters as directed.

	Diagnoses	ICD-10-CM	ICD-9-CM
1.	Lupus erythematosus		695.4
2.	Ingrown right great toenail		703.0
3.	Puncture of skin while treating dermatitis, accidental		998.2
4.	Right forearm cellulitis		
5.	Bullous impetigo		
6.	Stage 2 healing pressure ulcer, right elbow		
7.	Chronic urticaria		
8.	Senear-Usher syndrome		
9.	Puritus ani		
10.	Diaper rash		
11.	Acne vulgaris		
12.	Pityriasis rosea		
13.	Stage 2 healing pressure ulcer, right hip		
14.	Eczema		
15.	Boil, left buttock		
16.	Second degree sunburn of the back		
17.	Irritation dermatitis from contact with nickel in ring		
18.	Folliculitis, left cheek		
19.	Dermatitis from the sun		
20.	Keloid scar, lower left abdomen		
21.	Sebaceous cyst		
22.	Contact dermatitis from allergy to dog hair		
23.	Alopecia universalis		
24.	Rhinophyma		
25.	Chronic venous hypertension with right calf ulcer exposing muscle necrosis		

Diseases of the Musculoskeletal System and Connective Tissue (M00–M99)

Chapter 13 begins with a note to use the external cause code following the musculoskeletal condition code, if applicable; and an extensive list of "excludes 2" conditions that appear in other chapters.

Review and observe these exclusions when coding musculoskeletal and connective tissue disorders.

This chapter contains the following blocks:

M00–M02	Infectious arthropathies
M05–M14	Inflammatory polyarthropathies
M15–M19	Osteoarthritis
M20–M25	Other joint disorders
M26–M27	Dentofacial anomalies (including malocclusion) and other disorders of jaw
M30–M36	Systemic connective tissue disorders
M40–M43	Deforming dorsopathies
M45–M49	Spondylopathies
M50–M54	Other dorsopathies
M60–M63	Disorders of muscles
M65–M67	Disorders of synovium and tendon
M70–M79	Other soft tissue disorders
M80–M85	Disorders of bone density and structure
M86–M90	Other osteopathies
M91–M94	Chondropathies
M95	Other disorders of the musculoskeletal system and connective tissue
M96	Intraoperative and postprocedural complications and disorders of musculoskeletal system, not elsewhere classified
M99	Biomechanical lesions, not elsewhere classified

There are additional instructions within each block of codes advising "includes," "excludes 1," "excludes 2" "code first," "use additional code," or "code also." Code only what is stated or known in the medical record. If no additional information is provided in the worksheet, code only the specific term(s).

Name ______________________

Using the blocks on the previous page as guidance, locate the three-character categories for the following diagnoses:

	Diagnoses	ICD-10-CM	ICD-9-CM
1.	Acute gout	________	________
2.	Osteoarthritis, right knee, following a fall	________	________
3.	Calcium in the bursa, left ankle	________	________
4.	Legg-Calve-Perthes, right leg	________	________
5.	Effusion, left elbow	________	________
6.	Right foot rheumatoid arthritis nodule	________	________
7.	Left tennis elbow	________	________
8.	Lumbar kissing spine	________	________
9.	Single bone cyst, right humerus	________	________
10.	Left lumbago and sciatica	________	________

Name ____________________

Diseases of the Musculoskeletal System and Connective Tissue (M00–M99)

Using the alphabetic and tabular references, locate the following conditions and code to acceptable specificity, three to seven characters. Observe the coding instructions and include codes from other chapters as directed.

	Diagnoses	ICD-10-CM	ICD-9-CM
1.	Tendon contracture, right upper arm		
2.	Chronic gout, right big toe, cause unknown		
3.	Recurrent left knee dislocation		
4.	Lumbosacral scoliosis from cerebral palsy		
5.	Low back pain		
6.	Pneumococcal arthritis, right wrist		
7.	Dry socket left lower jaw		
8.	Trigger finger, right middle finger		
9.	Left wrist ganglion		
10.	Left hand synovitis from excessive rugby		
11.	Systemic lupus erythematosus		
12.	Cervical vertebral osteomyelitis		
13.	Arthropathy, left elbow, following gastric bypass		
14.	Consult for stress fracture, thoracic vertebra		
15.	Partial tear of left rotator cuff		
16.	Rupture of right wrist synovial cyst		
17.	Flat feet, not congenital		
18.	Fibromyalgia		
19.	Bursitis, right knee		
20.	Rheumatoid arthritis with myopathy, right hand		
21.	Old, well healed, collapsed cervical vertebral fracture		
22.	Radiculopathy L5-S1		
23.	Recurrent muscle spasms, left calf		
24.	Postlaminectomy kyphosis		
25.	ER visit for old-age osteoporosis and pathological fracture of right hip		

Name ____________________

Diseases of the Genitourinary System (N00–N99)

Chapter 14 begins with an extensive list of "excludes 2" conditions that appear in other chapters. Review and observe these exclusions when coding genitourinary disorders.

This chapter contains the following blocks:

N00–N08	Glomerular diseases
N10–N19	Renal tubulo-interstitial diseases
N17–N19	Acute kidney failure and chronic kidney disease
N20–N23	Urolithiasis
N25–N29	Other disorders of kidney and ureter
N30–N39	Other diseases of the urinary system
N40–N53	Diseases of male genital organs
N60–N65	Disorders of breast
N70–N77	Inflammatory diseases of female pelvis organs
N80–N98	Noninflammatory disorders of female genital tract
N99	Intraoperative and posprocedural complications and disorders of genitourinary system, not elsewhere classified

There are additional instructions within each block of codes advising "Includes," "excludes 1," "excludes 2," "code first," "use additional code," or "code also." Code only what is stated or known in the medical record. If no additional information is provided in the worksheet, code only the specific term(s).

Using the above blocks as guidance, locate the three-character categories for the following diagnoses:

Diagnoses	ICD-10-CM	ICD-9-CM
1. Overactive bladder	______	596.51
2. Acute prostatitis	______	601.0
3. Fibrocystic breast disease	______	610.1
4. Infertility from tubal stenosis	______	______
5. Glomerulonephritis	______	______
6. Kidney stone	______	______
7. Bertholin's gland cyst	______	______
8. Testicular atrophy	______	______
9. Paraphimosis	______	______
10. Metrorrhagia	______	______

Name ______________________

Diseases of the Genitourinary System (N00–N99)

Using the alphabetic and tabular references, locate the following conditions and code to acceptable specificity, three to seven characters. Observe the coding instructions and include codes from other chapters as directed.

	Diagnoses	ICD-10-CM	ICD-9-CM
1.	Stage 2 chronic kidney disease	______	______
2.	Asymptomatic enlarged prostate	______	______
3.	Chronic salpingo-oophoritis	______	______
4.	Paravaginal cystocele	______	______
5.	Breast lump	______	______
6.	Nocturnal enuresis	______	______
7.	Cystostomy stoma malfunction	______	______
8.	Acute cystitis, no hematuria	______	______
9.	Male stress incontinence	______	______
10.	Encysted hydrocele	______	______
11.	Uterine endometriosis	______	______
12.	Nephroptosis	______	______
13.	Posthysterectomy vaginal vault prolapsed	______	______
14.	Urethral stricture from injury, 42-year-old male	______	______
15.	Acute glomerulonephritis	______	______
16.	Chronic uremia	______	______
17.	Hydronephrosis	______	______
18.	Misshapen left breast following reconstruction	______	______
19.	Primary amenorrhea	______	______
20.	Pelvic inflammatory disease	______	______
21.	Painful erection	______	______
22.	Mittelschmerz	______	______
23.	Ovarian hyperstimulation from induced ovulation	______	______
24.	Senile atrophic vaginitis	______	______
25.	Absolute male infertility	______	______

Name ____________________

Pregnancy, Childbirth, and the Puerperium (O00-O9A)

Chapter 15 begins with notes that (1) these codes are only used on maternal records, and (2) trimesters are counted from the first day after the last menstrual period. There is a note that pregnancy requires a code from category Z3A to identify the specific week of pregnancy. Review also the "excludes 1" and "excludes 2" notes.

This chapter contains the following blocks:

O00-O08	Pregnancy with abortive outcome
O09	Supervision of high-risk pregnancy
O10–O16	Edema, proteinuria and hypertensive disorders in pregnancy, childbirth and the puerperium
020–O29	Other maternal disorders predominantly related to pregnancy
O30–O48	Maternal care related to the fetus and amniotic cavity and possible delivery problems
O60–O77	Complications of labor and delivery
O80–O82	Encounter for delivery
O85–092	Complications predominantly related to the puerperium
O94–O9A	Other obstetric conditions not elsewhere classified

There are additional instructions within each block of codes advising "includes," "excludes 1," "excludes 2," "code first," "code also," or use additional code." Code only what is stated or known in the medical record. If no additional information is provided in the worksheet, code only the specific term(s).

Using the above blocks as guidance, locate the three-character categories for the following diagnoses:

	Diagnoses	ICD-10-CM	ICD-9-CM
1.	Fallopian pregnancy	________	633.11
2.	Mild hyperemesis gravidarum, 17 weeks	________	643.00
3.	Spontaneous miscarriage	________	634.90
4.	Abnormal prenatal chromosome lab test	________	________
5.	Bladder infection of pregnancy	________	________
6.	Braxton Hicks contractions	________	________
7.	Prenatal deep-vein thrombosis	________	________
8.	Shock following induced abortion	________	________
9.	Pregnancy complicated by physical abuse, 16-year-old	________	________
10.	Gestational diabetes mellitus	________	________

Name ____________________

Pregnancy, Childbirth, and the Puerperium (O00–O9A)

Using the alphabetic and tabular references, locate the following conditions and code to acceptable specificity, three to seven characters. Observe the coding instructions and include codes from other chapters as directed.

	Diagnoses	ICD-10-CM	ICD-9-CM
1.	Uterine rupture during labor		
2.	Delivery of triplets by Cesarean Section, all liveborn		
3.	Excessive weight gain, 29 weeks		
4.	Placenta previa with hemorrhage, 19 weeks		641.13
5.	Partial hydatidiform mole		630.
6.	Triplet pregnancy, 24 weeks		651.13
7.	Manage high-risk pregnancy, first trimester (previous stillborn)		
8.	Failed termination of pregnancy with hemorrhage		
9.	Acute kidney failure after spontaneous abortion		
10.	Normal pregnancy, delivery of live male infant		
11.	Cracked nipple from lactation		
12.	UTI after incomplete miscarriage		
13.	Preterm labor, delivery of female infant at term, 30 weeks		
14.	Husband's psychological abuse complicates 25 week pregnancy		
15.	Uremia following ectopic pregnancy		
16.	Two-pack a day cigarette use, complicating pregnancy		
17.	Renal shutdown following induced termination		
18.	Age 15, supervision of third pregnancy, 17 weeks		
19.	Precipitate labor		
20.	Cardiomyopathy developed in third trimester		
21.	Cord entanglement making labor and delivery difficult		
22.	Hemorrhoids of pregnancy, 15 weeks		
23.	Postpartum hemorrhoids		
24.	Normal OB care, first trimester		
25.	Missed abortion, 16 weeks		

Certain Conditions Originating in the Perinatal Period (P00–P96)

Chapter 16 begins with a note that these codes are used only on newborn records, never on maternal records. There is an "includes" note defining conditions that originate in the fetal or perinatal period (through the first 28 days after birth even if the morbidity occurs later). Review the extensive list of "excludes 2" conditions that appear in other chapters. Review and observe these directions when coding this chapter.

This chapter contains the following blocks:

P00–P04	Newborn affected by maternal factors and by complications of pregnancy, labor, and delivery
P05–P08	Disorder of newborn related to length of gestation and fetal growth
P09	Abnormal findings on neonatal screening
P10–P15	Birth trauma
P19–P29	Respiratory and cardiovascular disorders specific to the perinatal period
P35–P39	Infections specific to the perinatal period
P50–P61	Hemorrhagic and hematological disorders of newborn
P70–P74	Transitory endocrine and metabolic disorders specific to newborn
P76–P78	Digestive system disorders of newborn
P80–P83	Conditions involving the integument and temperature regulation of newborn
P84	Other problems with newborn
P90–P96	Other disorders originating in the perinatal period

There are additional instructions within each block of codes advising "includes," "excludes 1," "excludes 2," "code first," "code also," or "use additional code." Code only what is stated or known in the medical record. If no additional information is provided in the worksheet, code only the specific term(s).

Name ______________________

Using the blocks on the previous page as guidance, locate the three-character categories for the following diagnoses:

	Diagnoses	ICD-10-CM	ICD-9-CM
1.	Crack baby	________	760.75
2.	Newborn possibly affected by amniocentesis	________	760.61
3.	Wet lung syndrome	________	518.52
4.	Polycythemia neonatorum	________	776.4
5.	Localized subdural hematoma from birth injury	________	________
6.	Failure to thrive in 14-day-old male	________	________
7.	Prematurity hyperbilirubinemia	________	________
8.	Pneumonia secondary to aspiration of blood	________	________
9.	Newborn weighing 10.2 lbs.	________	________
10.	Fetal chignon from vacuum extractor	________	________

Name ____________________

Certain Conditions Originating in the Perinatal Period (P00–P96)

Using the alphabetic and tabular references, locate the following conditions and code to acceptable specificity, three to seven characters. Observe the coding instructions and include codes from other chapters as directed.

	Diagnoses	ICD-10-CM	ICD-9-CM
1.	Maternal death suspected to affect newborn		
2.	Meconium aspiration pneumonia		
3.	Small-for-dates newborn, 5.1 lbs.		
4.	Newborn vitamin K deficiency		
5.	Congenital rubella pneumonitis		
6.	Infant-of-a-diabetic-mother syndrome		
7.	Stillborn infant		
8.	Cesarian delivery perhaps affecting newborn		
9.	Newborn *Staphylococcus aureus* sepsis		
10.	Possible impact on newborn from tight cord around neck		
11.	Post-term newborn, 41 weeks		
12.	Newborn 32 weeks, weighting 3.1 pounds		
13.	Neonatal bruising with jaundice		
14.	Obstructive newborn apnea		
15.	Newborn regurgitation/rumination		
16.	Bradycardia in newborn		
17.	Grey baby syndrome		
18.	Meconiun ileus		
19.	Perinatal pneumothorax		
20.	Congenital toxoplasmosis		
21.	Mother is cocaine dependent, newborn has withdrawal symptoms		
22.	Facial palsy from birth injury		
23.	Wilson-Mikity syndrome		
24.	Newborn may be affected by abruptio placenta		
25.	Newborn hypoxia		

Name ______________________

Congenital Malformations, Deformations, and Chromosomal Abnormalities (Q00–Q99)

Chapter 17 begins with a note that codes from this chapter are not used on maternal or fetal records. There is an "excludes 2" reference to inborn errors of metabolism. Review and observe these notes and exclusions when coding this chapter.

This chapter contains the following blocks:

Q00–Q07	Congenital malformations of the nervous system
Q10–Q18	Congenital malformations of eye, ear, face, and neck
Q20–Q28	Congenital malformations of the circulatory system
Q30–Q34	Congenital malformations of the respiratory system
Q35–Q37	Cleft lip and cleft palate
Q38–Q45	Other congenital malformations of the digestive system
Q50–Q56	Congenital malformations of genital organs
Q60–Q64	Congenital malformations of the urinary system
Q65–Q79	Congenital malformations and deformations of the musculoskeletal system
Q80–Q89	Other congenital malformations
Q90–Q99	Chromosomal abnormalities, not elsewhere classified

There are additional instructions within each block of codes advising "includes," "excludes 1," "excludes 2," "code first," "code also," or "use additional code." Code only what is stated or known in the medical record. If no additional information is provided in the worksheet, code only the specific term(s).

Using the above blocks as guidance, locate the three-character categories for the following diagnoses:

	Diagnoses	ICD-10-CM	ICD-9-CM
1.	Congenital absence of the outer ear	________	________
2.	Congenital partial dislocation of left hip	________	________
3.	Dandy-Walker syndrome	________	________
4.	Tetralogy of Fallot	________	________
5.	Ankyloglossia	________	________
6.	Bicornate uterus	________	________
7.	Harelip	________	________
8.	Supernumerary ear	________	________
9.	Strawberry nevus	________	________
10.	Polydactyly	________	________

Name ______________________

Congenital Malformations, Deformations, and Chromosomal Abnormalities (Q00–Q99)

Using the alphabetic and tabular references, locate the following conditions and code to acceptable specificity, three to seven characters. Observe the coding instructions and include codes from other chapters as directed.

	Diagnoses	ICD-10-CM	ICD-9-CM
1.	Fragile X syndrome	________	________
2.	Congenital aortic insufficiency	________	________
3.	Penile hypospadias	________	________
4.	Stenosis of aqueduct of Sylvius	________	________
5.	Bilateral webbed toes	________	________
6.	Harlequin fetus	________	________
7.	Hereditary cystic lung disease	________	________
8.	Trisomy 21, IQ 40–50	________	________
9.	Acrocephaly	________	________
10.	Cleft soft palate and bilateral cleft lip	________	________
11.	Lumbosacral spina bifida, no hydrocephalus	________	________
12.	Congenital absence of both lower limbs	________	________
13.	Arnold-Chiari syndrome and spina bifida	________	________
14.	Congenital AV aneurysm pulmonary artery	________	________
15.	Spina bifida occulta	________	________
16.	Congenital right cataract	________	________
17.	Von Recklinghausen disease	________	________
18.	Autosomal recessive polycystic kidney disease	________	________
19.	Microgastria	________	________
20.	Patent ductus arteriosus	________	________
21.	Congenital pancreatic agenesis	________	________
22.	Congenital talipes equinovarus	________	________
23.	Sponge kidney	________	________
24.	Dextrocardia	________	________
25.	Prune-belly syndrome	________	________

Symptoms, Signs, and Abnormal Clinical and Laboratory Findings, Not Elsewhere Classified (R00–R99)

Chapter 18 begins with long note on the uses of these codes and a list of "excludes 2" conditions that appear in other chapters. Review and observe all notes and exclusions when coding this chapter.

This chapter contains the following blocks:

R00–R09	Symptoms and signs involving the circulatory and respiratory systems
R10–R19	Symptoms and signs involving the digestive system and abdomen
R20–R23	Symptoms and signs involving the skin and subcutaneous tissue
R25–R29	Symptoms and signs involving the nervous and musculoskeletal systems
R30–R39	Symptoms and signs involving the genitourinary system
R40–R46	Symptoms and signs involving cognition, perceptions, emotional state, and behavior
R47–R49	Symptoms and signs involving speech and voice
R50–R69	General symptoms and signs
R70–R77	Abnormal findings on examination of blood without diagnosis
R80–R82	Abnormal finding on examination of urine without diagnosis
R83–R89	Abnormal findings on examination of other body fluids, substances, and tissues without diagnosis
R90–R94	Abnormal findings on diagnostic imaging and in function studies without diagnosis
R97	Abnormal tumor markers
R99	Ill-defined and unknown cause of mortality

There are additional instructions within each block of codes advising "includes," "excludes 1," "excludes 2," "code first," "code also," or "use additional code." Code only what is stated or known in the medical record. If no additional information is provided in the worksheet, code only the specific term(s).

Name ______________________

Using the blocks on the previous page as guidance, locate the three-character categories for the following diagnoses:

Diagnoses	ICD-10-CM	ICD-9-CM
1. Slow heart beat	________	________
2. Hoarseness	________	________
3. Cheyne-Stokes respiration	________	________
4. Elevated fasting glucose	________	________
5. Bilious emesis	________	________
6. Anterior chest-wall pain	________	________
7. Memory loss	________	________
8. Occult blood in stools	________	________
9. Lymphadenopathy	________	________
10. Anhedonia	________	________

Name ____________________

Symptoms, Signs, and Abnormal Clinical and Laboratory Findings, Not Elsewhere Classified (R00–R99)

Using the alphabetic and tabular references, locate the following conditions and code to acceptable specificity, three to seven characters. Observe the coding instructions and include codes from other chapters as directed.

	Diagnoses	ICD-10-CM	ICD-9-CM
1.	Severe sepsis with shock	________	________
2.	Periumbilical pain	________	________
3.	Vertigo	________	________
4.	Elevated blood pressure, no hypertension	________	________
5.	Abnormal cervical Pap smear	________	________
6.	Headache	________	________
7.	Chronic peritoneal effusion	________	________
8.	Excessive crying, 12-day-old infant	________	________
9.	Intellectual functioning at borderline level	________	________
10.	Localized edema, right foot	________	________
11.	Flatulence	________	________
12.	Postnasal drip	________	________
13.	Fasciculations of lower extremities	________	________
14.	Hemoptysis	________	________
15.	Frequent blushing	________	________
16.	Swollen lump or mass, right neck	________	________
17.	Physical debility from old age	________	________
18.	Functional urinary incontinence	________	________
19.	Cardiorespiratory failure	________	________
20.	Chronic fatigue syndrome	________	________
21.	Skin induration	________	________
22.	Abnormal EEG	________	________
23.	Persistent vegetative state	________	________
24.	Postimmunization fever	________	________
25.	Painful urination	________	________

Injury, Poisoning, and Certain Other Consequences of External Causes (S00–T88)

When coding **Chapter 19**, review and observe all notes, instructions, and exclusions. These codes frequently require a code from another Chapter.

This chapter contains the following blocks:

S00–S09	Injuries to the head
S10–S19	Injuries to the neck
S20–S29	Injuries to the thorax
S30–S39	Injuries to the abdomen, lower back, lumbar spine, pelvis, and external genitals
S40–S49	Injuries to the shoulder and upper arm
S50–S59	Injuries to the elbow and forearm
S60–S69	Injuries to the wrist, hand, and fingers
S70–S79	Injuries to the hip and thigh
S80–S89	Injuries to the knee and lower leg
S90–S99	Injuries to the ankle and foot
T07	Injuries involving multiple body regions
T14	Injury to unspecified body region
T15–T19	Effects of foreign body entering through natural orifice
T20–T25	Burns and corrosions of external body surface, specified by site
T26–T28	Burns and corrosions confined to eye and internal organs
T30–T32	Burns and corrosions of multiple and unspecified body regions
T33–T34	Frostbite
T36–T50	Poisoning by or adverse effect of an underdosing of drugs, medicaments, and biological substances
T51–T65	Toxic effects of substances chiefly nonmedicinal as to source
T66–T78	Other and unspecified effects of external causes
T79	Certain early complications of trauma
T80–T88	Complications of surgical and medical care, not elsewhere classified

There are additional instructions within each block of codes, advising "includes," "excludes 1," "excludes 2," "code first," "code also," or "use additional code." Code only what is stated or known in the medical record. If no additional information is provided in the worksheet, code only the specific term(s).

Name ___________________________

Using the blocks on the previous page as guidance, locate the three-character categories for the following diagnoses:

Diagnoses	ICD-10-CM	ICD-9-CM
1. Scalp laceration with foreign body	________	________
2. New bucket-handle tear, right medial meniscus	________	________
3. Death from concussion with no return to consciousness	________	________
4. Aero-otitis media	________	________
5. Fracture of lumbosacral vertebra	________	________
6. Rejection of bone marrow transplant	________	________
7. Nondisplaced fracture, body of left scapula	________	________
8. First-degree burn of elbow, right	________	________
9. Superficial frostbite of the nose	________	________
10. Posterior arch fracture, first cervical vertebra	________	________

Name ______________________

Injury, Poisoning, and Certain Other Consequences of External Causes (S00–T88)

Using the alphabetic and tabular references, locate the following conditions and code to acceptable specificity, three to seven characters. Observe the coding instructions and include codes from other chapters as directed. Unless otherwise specified, all encounters are "initial."

	Diagnoses	ICD-10-CM	ICD-9-CM
1.	Lump from nonvenomous insect bite, 1 year ago, left breast	________	________
2.	Rejection of lung transplant	________	________
3.	Seen again for nonunion, torus fracture, left lower fibula	________	________
4.	ER visit for Type IIIA fracture, left femur neck	________	________
5.	Foreign body, left cornea	________	________
6.	Left ankle sprain	________	________
7.	Follow up for FB accidentally left in from heart cath	________	________
8.	Cervical spine nerve root injury	________	________
9.	Per police report and confirmed by physician: Elderly patient abused by home health care worker	________	________
10.	Black eye, right, follow up visit	________	________
11.	Fracture mandibular ramus, healing well	________	________
12.	Foreign body (stone) in left nostril	________	________
13.	Continuing care for subluxation L4/L5 vertebra	________	________
14.	Rash at site of immunization	________	________
15.	ER visit, suicide attempt with aspirin	________	________
16.	Third degree burn, left palm	________	________
17.	Traumatic partial amputation right ear, 20 minutes ago	________	________
18.	Necrotic frostbite, left ear	________	________
19.	Seen for sequelae of toxic cobra venom	________	________
20.	Seen again for nasal bone fracture	________	________
21.	Third visit for allergic reaction	________	________
22.	Accidental poisoning by shellfish	________	________
23.	Crush injury, right great toe	________	________
24.	Seen for left shoulder puncture with foreign body	________	________
25.	Seen in ER for esophageal burn from coffee she drank	________	________

External Causes of Morbidity (V00–Y99)

Chapter 20 has extensive notes on the proper use of these codes with other chapter conditions. Observe all Chapter 20 instructions and guidelines. These codes replace the "E" codes of ICD-9-CM. Use of these codes may point to billing a liability carrier or auto insurance rather than the patient's private health insurance.

This chapter contains the following blocks:

V00–Y09	Pedestrian injured in transport accident
V10–V19	Pedal cycle rider injured in transport accident
V20–V29	Motorcycle rider injured in transport accident
V30–V39	Occupant of three-wheeled motor vehicle injured in transport accident
V40–V49	Car occupant injured in transport accident
V50–V59	Occupant of pick-up truck or van injured in transport accident
V60–V69	Occupant of heavy transport vehicle injured in transport accident
V70–V79	Bus occupant injured in transport accident
V80–V89	Other land transport accidents
V90–V94	Water transport accidents
V95–V97	Air and space transport accidents
V98–V99	Other and unspecified transport accidents
W00–X58	Other external causes of accidental injury
W00–W19	Slipping, tripping, stumbling and falls
W20–W49	Exposure to inanimate mechanical forces
W50–W64	Exposure to animate mechanical forces
W65–W74	Accidental non-transport drowning and submersion
W85–W99	Exposure to electric current, radiation and extreme ambient air temperature and pressure
X00–X08	Exposure to smoke, fire and flames
X10–X19	Contact with heat and hot substances
X30–X39	Exposure to forces of nature
X52–X58	Accidental exposure to other specified factors
X71–X83	Intentional self-harm
X92–Y08	Assault
Y21–Y33	Event of undetermined intent
Y35–Y38	Legal intervention, operations of war, military operations, and terrorism
Y62–Y84	Complications of medical and surgical care
Y62–Y69	Misadventures to patients during surgical and medical care
Y70–Y82	Medical devices associated with adverse incidents in diagnostic and therapeutic use
Y83–Y84	Surgical and other medical procedures as the cause of abnormal reaction of the patient, or of later complication, without mention of misadventure at the time of the procedure
Y90–Y99	Supplementary factors related to causes of morbidity classified elsewhere

Name ________________________

Code only what is stated or known in the medical record. If no additional information is provided in the worksheet, code only the specific term(s).

Using the blocks on the previous page as guidance, locate the three-character categories for the following diagnoses:

	Diagnoses	ICD-10-CM	ICD-9-CM
1.	Snowboarder collided with a tree	____________	E848
2.	Two dune buggies collided, one passenger injured	____________	E821.1-
3.	Paper cut	____________	____________
4.	Bystander injured when police used tear gas	____________	____________
5.	Right leg amputated: wrong leg	____________	____________
6.	Injured while running with scissors	____________	____________
7.	Bitten by a macaw	____________	____________
8.	Toddler fell out when grocery cart tipped over	____________	____________
9.	Injured when a small plane hit his car	____________	____________
10.	Runner injured in Boston Marathon bombing	____________	____________

Name ____________________

External Causes of Morbidity (V00–Y99)

Using the alphabetic and tabular references, locate the following conditions and code to acceptable specificity, three to seven characters. Observe the coding instructions and include the location and activity codes (Y92–Y99) if applicable for initial service. These codes may not be used as the principle diagnosis and may not be required at present. We need to learn to use them correctly in case they are mandated in the future. All are the "initial encounter."

	Diagnoses	ICD-10-CM	Location/Activity
1.	Nanny with a baby stroller was injured by a bicyclist in the park	________	________
2.	Struck by baseball at high school home game	________	________
3.	Injured in an avalanche	________	________
4.	Armored car driver injured in collision with a cow	________	________
5.	Injured in his garage workshop by his radial saw	________	________
6.	Driver of fork lift injured in a warehouse accident	________	________
7.	Foster mother neglected and mistreated the toddler	________	________
8.	Occupant injured when train collided with military truck	________	________
9.	Car passenger injured at intersection collision with SUV	________	________
10.	Sawed off ring causing constriction to her finger	________	________
11.	Bitten by an orca while surfing in the ocean	________	________
12.	Fell from icy steps at local grocery store	________	________
13.	Snowmobile driver injured in collision with moving car	________	________
14.	Burned when the kayak caught fire on the river	________	________
15.	Dove into the lake, struck the bottom, and drowned	________	________
16.	Child accidentally drowned, left alone in bathtub	________	________
17.	Canoer hurt when hit by motorboat	________	________
18.	Became ill from smoke and fumes when his apartment caught fire	________	________
19.	Hurt left hand while playing racquetball	________	________
20.	Injuries occurred when he fell off the toilet at his apartment	________	________
21.	Bulldozer driver injured when earth collapsed under him	________	________
22.	Child hurt when IED exploded; war souvenir from Iraq	________	________
23.	Injured from exposure to tanning bed	________	________
24.	Was assaulted and struck by a hockey stick	________	________
25.	Fell asleep smoking, setting hotel sofa on fire	________	________

Factors Influencing Health Status and Contact with Health Services (Z00–Z99)

Chapter 21 begins with an explanation that these codes represent reasons for encounters and that a corresponding procedure code must accompany a Z code if a procedure from other chapters is performed. Review and observe all notes, exclusions, and chapter guidelines when coding this chapter. These codes expand the "V" codes in ICD-9-CM.

This chapter contains the following blocks:

Z00–Z13	Persons encountering health service for examinations
Z14–Z15	Genetic carrier and genetic susceptibility to disease
Z16	Resistance to antimicrobial drugs
Z17	Estrogen receptor status
Z18	Retained foreign body fragments
Z20–Z28	Persons with potential health hazards related to communicable diseases
Z30–Z39	Persons encountering health services in circumstances related to reproduction
Z40–Z53	Encounters for other specific health care
Z55–Z65	Persons with potential health hazards related to socioeconomic and psychosocial circumstances
Z66	Do not resuscitate status
Z67	Blood type
Z68	Body mass index (BMI)
Z69–Z76	Persons encountering health services in other circumstances
Z77–Z99	Persons with potential health hazards related to family and personal history and certain conditions influencing health status

There are additional instructions within each block of codes advising "includes," "excludes 1," "excludes 2," "code first," "code also," or "use additional code." Code only what is stated or known in the medical record. If no additional information is provided in the worksheet, code only the specific term(s).

Name ______________________

Using the blocks on the previous page as guidance, locate the three-character categories for the following diagnoses:

	Diagnoses	ICD-10-CM	ICD-9-CM
1.	Physical exam for summer camp	________	V70.3
2.	Seen for suture removal	________	V58.32
3.	Family history of alcohol dependence/abuse	________	________
4.	Encounter for exam of ears and hearing evaluation	________	________
5.	Has used insulin for the past 22 years	________	________
6.	Visit to enroll patient in palliative care	________	________
7.	Personal history of thrombophlebitis	________	________
8.	Immunization declined based on religion	________	________
9.	Empty nest syndrome	________	________
10.	Seen for consideration of breast implants	________	________

Name ___________________________

Factors Influencing Health Status and Contact with Health Services (Z00–Z99)

Using the alphabetic and tabular references, locate the following conditions and code to acceptable specificity, three to seven characters. Observe the coding instructions and chapter-specific guidelines. These are initial visits unless otherwise specified. Include codes from other chapters, as directed, if that information is included.

	Diagnoses	ICD-10-CM	ICD-9-CM
1.	Routine GYN exam, without abnormal findings	____________	____________
2.	Encounter for postmastectomy breast reconstruction	____________	____________
3.	Seen for inability to get along with boss and workmates	____________	____________
4.	Type O blood, Rh negative	____________	____________
5.	Has Alzheimer's and needs continuous supervision	____________	____________
6.	Encounter for pregnancy test with positive result	____________	____________
7.	Type A behavior pattern	____________	____________
8.	Genetic susceptibility to breast cancer	____________	____________
9.	Gastric bypass status for obesity	____________	____________
10.	Observation for suspected ingestion of poison, ruled out	____________	____________
11.	Had polio as a child	____________	____________
12.	Personal history of basal and squamous cell CA	____________	____________
13.	Seen to screen for diabetes mellitus	____________	____________
14.	Visit to fit and adjust artificial left eye	____________	____________
15.	Worried about possible loan foreclosure on home	____________	____________
16.	Adult body mass index: 23.5	____________	____________
17.	Issuing repeat prescriptions for a chronic disease	____________	____________
18.	High-risk bisexual behavior	____________	____________
19.	Visit to determine Rh incompatibility status	____________	____________
20.	Contact with and exposure to asbestos	____________	____________
21.	Patient has resistance to ampicillin	____________	____________
22.	Rape victim seen for counseling	____________	____________
23.	Status post total hysterectomy	____________	____________
24.	Visit to screen for chlamydia	____________	____________
25.	Allergic to shellfish	____________	____________

Name ______________________

PUTTING IT ALL TOGETHER

This series of case studies asks you to find the correct procedure and diagnosis codes. Note also that you are asked to include any required modifier. The answers and the rationale for the answer follow this section. Read the case studies carefully, look for key terms, and be certain to follow all coding rules from CPT, HCPCS, and ICD-10-CM. List the procedures and modifiers in the order they would appear on the claim form (1–4) and list the corresponding diagnoses with numbers 1–4.

1. The patient has an unstable left keratoconus. He can no longer keep his contact lenses in place. The surgeon performed an anterior lamellar keratoplasty.

Proc/Mod			ICD-10-CM		
	1	____________		1	____________
	2	____________		2	____________
	3	____________		3	____________
	4	____________		4	____________

2. A 22-year-old male was admitted to a residential psychiatric facility for treatment of an exacerbation of Asperger's syndrome. Following a comprehensive workup, he had 30 minutes of biofeedback psychotherapy on the day of admission.

Proc/Mod			ICD-10-CM		
	1	____________		1	____________
	2	____________		2	____________
	3	____________		3	____________
	4	____________		4	____________

3. The physician admitted the patient to a nursing facility and performed a detailed history and physical examination with medical decision of low complexity. Mr. Roberts had recovered sufficiently from his left-sided paralysis following a stroke. Since he is right-handed, he can now feed and dress himself. Mr. Roberts has a mild residual monoplegia of the left lower leg.

Proc/Mod			ICD-10-CM		
	1	____________		1	____________
	2	____________		2	____________
	3	____________		3	____________
	4	____________		4	____________

Name ____________________

4. Dr. Jack Armstrong, an orthopedic surgeon, discharged Mary Martin from City Hospital following a right total hip replacement for osteoarthritis.

Proc/Mod		ICD-10-CM	
1	________	1	________
2	________	2	________
3	________	3	________
4	________	4	________

5. Michael Jaydan injured his left thumb playing basketball. He was seen in Dr. Spaulding's after hours urgent care center. The doctor performed a new patient EPF visit and took two x-ray views of the left thumb. There was no fracture. Dr. Spaulding treated the sprain injury by strapping the thumb with one yard of 3-inch elastic compression bandage.

Proc/Mod		ICD-10-CM	
1	________	1	________
2	________	2	________
3	________	3	________
4	________	4	________

6. Paul Brown, age 87, was scheduled at Metropolitan Hospital for outpatient surgery to replace his mature right cortical cataract with a lens implant. Just as Dr. Black was to begin the procedure, Mr. Brown developed a significant cardiac dysrhythmia. The surgery was canceled and Dr. Black admitted Mr. Brown to the hospital's observation unit for care of the arrhythmia. Dr. Green, a cardiologist, later that day admitted Mr. Brown to Metropolitan Hospital for a complete cardiac workup.

Code the services of Dr. Black.

Proc/Mod		ICD-10-CM	
1	________	1	________
2	________	2	________
3	________	3	________
4	________	4	________

7. An ambulance brought a 37-year-old man to the Central City Hospital ER after he was injured in a hit-and-run accident. The orthopedic surgeon, Dr. Frost, treated the patient in the emergency department for a fractured metacarpal, right ring finger; a fractured mandible on the right; and the closed treatment of a fractured right femur shaft. When the patient was stable, Dr. Robins admitted him to Central City Hospital for continuing care of the fractures. Code Dr. Frost's services.

Proc/Mod		ICD-10-CM	
1	________	1	________
2	________	2	________
3	________	3	________
4	________	4	________

Name ______________________

8. Dr. Dallas discharged 79-year-old Mary Stuart from Mercy Medical Center after she recovered from an extrinsic status asthmaticus attack. She was seen that afternoon in his office for wheezing that did not respond to a non-compounded 1 mg unit dose albuterol nebulizer treatment. She was readmitted to Mercy for further care of her acute asthma episode.

Proc/Mod			ICD-10-CM		
	1	________		1	________
	2	________		2	________
	3	________		3	________
	4	________		4	________

9. Jennifer Taylor, age 4, was seen by her osteopathic pediatrician after she had been ill for two days with a productive cough and now had developed a fever. Her examination focused on the presenting problems. The doctor diagnosed bronchitis and a somatic dysfunction of the cervical, thoracic, rib, and abdominal areas. She was treated with medication and OMT.

Proc/Mod			ICD-10-CM		
	1	________		1	________
	2	________		2	________
	3	________		3	________
	4	________		4	________

10. Harry Morgan, who has Type 2 diabetes and severe osteoarthritis, was seen to discuss his recent lab work. When he appeared uncoordinated and confused, Dr. Jessup did a glucose test with a reagent strip that showed Mr. Morgan's glucose level was low. Mr. Morgan was given crackers and a drink and later retested. Dr. Jessup became concerned that Harry was not taking his medications correctly or perhaps had developed a new problem, so he ordered a comprehensive metabolic panel. Mr. Morgan was in the office for over an hour and monitored closely by the doctor as documented in the medical record. The physician documents the diagnosis as: Type 2 DM with hypoglycemia.

Proc/Mod			ICD-10-CM		
	1	________		1	________
	2	________		2	________
	3	________		3	________
	4	________		4	________

Name ______________________

11. When Dr. Davis saw Ralph Cramer in a subsequent inpatient visit today, the patient stated he wanted to get out of the hospital in time for his granddaughter's birthday party tomorrow. His only complaints were some backache from spending a week in a hospital bed. The doctor ordered a final lab test to confirm that the severe urinary tract infection that required hospitalization was no longer present. Dr. Davis told Mr. Cramer he would return by noon tomorrow, and, if the lab work showed no problems, he would send him home at that time.

Proc/Mod			ICD-10-CM		
	1	____________		1	____________
	2	____________		2	____________
	3	____________		3	____________
	4	____________		4	____________

12. Fred Smith returned to his cardiologist's office for a 6-month recheck of the medications for his hypertensive heart disease. His EKG showed abnormalities, so Dr. Peck ordered a cardiovascular stress test to be done before Mr. Smith left the office. The doctor's physician assistant supervised the test and prepared the tracing for Dr. Peck's interpretation. The stress test revealed ischemia, possibly related to a recent "silent" myocardial infarction. Mr. Smith was scheduled for further workup.

Proc/Mod			ICD-10-CM		
	1	____________		1	____________
	2	____________		2	____________
	3	____________		3	____________
	4	____________		4	____________

13. A male patient was seen in his family doctor's office as an emergency. He was treated with a stinging insect venom injection for anaphylaxis, secondary to a bee sting.

Proc/Mod			ICD-10-CM		
	1	____________		1	____________
	2	____________		2	____________
	3	____________		3	____________
	4	____________		4	____________

Name ____________________

14. A 19-year-old male took his girlfriend hunting. Her shotgun accidentally discharged in the duck blind, and he was hit just below the right eye by a ricocheted shot. He had no change in vision but did have a small laceration and bruising in the area. Films in the emergency department revealed a metal foreign body embedded in the right eyelid just above the laceration. The cheek laceration was sutured and the foreign body removed by the ER physician. The patient was advised to see his primary care physician for follow-up care. The gunshot accident was reported to the authorities. The foreign body was given to the patient, who wanted it as a "souvenir."

Proc/Mod			ICD-10-CM		
	1	____________		1	____________
	2	____________		2	____________
	3	____________		3	____________
	4	____________		4	____________

15. A 37-year-old new patient was seen in the office for trauma to the left elbow received in a fall. X-rays (two views) of the elbow revealed no fracture. The patient was advised to rest the arm and use hot or cold compresses on the swelling, depending on which made it feel better. He was asked to contact the office if the arm was not better in a few days. As the patient was about to leave the exam room, he asked the doctor to remove the impacted cerumen from both ears. This was done with a curette and lavage.

Proc/Mod			ICD-10-CM		
	1	____________		1	____________
	2	____________		2	____________
	3	____________		3	____________
	4	____________		4	____________

16. Dr. Brady, a pediatrician in solo practice, performed a routine newborn exam on Baby Boy Peterson. Later that day the baby developed a severe, but not critical, respiratory distress and was transferred to the care of Dr. Lewis, a neonatologist, who admitted the baby to the neonatal intensive care unit (NICU).

Dr.Brady's services:

Proc/Mod			ICD-10-CM		
	1	____________		1	____________
	2	____________		2	____________

Dr. Lewis's services:

Proc/Mod			ICD-10-CM		
	1	____________		1	____________
	2	____________		2	____________

Name ____________________

17. The client was seen in a full 60-minute psychotherapy visit for a posttraumatic stress disorder. Dr. Bauer asked her to stay longer for biofeedback training to help her nicotine dependence and to stop cigarette smoking and to reduce stress.

Proc/Mod			ICD-10-CM		
	1	________		1	________
	2	________		2	________
	3	________		3	________
	4	________		4	________

18. Dr. Franklin left a group practice in East Jordan and set up private practice in Summerville, a town about 25 miles west of East Jordan. Some of her patients followed her to the new practice. She set up new records for these patients and incorporated copies from the group practice records into these charts. She saw Robert Taylor from her prior practice for an expanded problem focused visit and for the 6-month renewal of his prescriptions for Type 2 diabetes.

Proc/Mod			ICD-10-CM		
	1	________		1	________
	2	________		2	________
	3	________		3	________
	4	________		4	________

19. The 13-year-old patient had an abscess on the right middle finger and a sebaceous cyst of the left first toe. Both lesions were treated by I & D at the same operative session.

Proc/Mod			ICD-10-CM		
	1	________		1	________
	2	________		2	________
	3	________		3	________
	4	________		4	________

20. John Williams, a 59-year-old real estate agent, complained of occasional rectal bleeding over the past year. He was scheduled for a diagnostic flexible sigmoidoscopy. The surgeon also removed three polyps using bipolar cautery. Two polyps were removed intact while the third polyp had to be removed piecemeal. All lesions were proximal to the splenic flexure.

Proc/Mod			ICD-10-CM		
	1	________		1	________
	2	________		2	________
	3	________		3	________
	4	________		4	________

Name ______________________

21. Frank Johnson had worsening pain in his right knee over the past year. Dr. Butler performed a diagnostic arthroscopy with a partial medial meniscectomy and chondroplasty of two compartments of the right knee for osteochondritis.

Proc/Mod			ICD-10-CM		
	1	________		1	________
	2	________		2	________
	3	________		3	________
	4	________		4	________

22. The emergency room doctor at City Hospital diagnosed a 19-week missed abortion for Martha Thomas. She had a D&C and subsequently delivered all the products of conception.

Proc/Mod			ICD-10-CM		
	1	________		1	________
	2	________		2	________
	3	________		3	________
	4	________		4	________

23. George Smith had not seen Dr. Mann for two years when he returned to the office concerned about some "red bumps" on his face, neck, and arms. During the EPF visit, Dr. Mann diagnosed the "bumps" as actinic keratoses. The doctor also removed a skin tag from the neck or shoulder area where it had been irritated by Mr. Smith's shirt collars.

Proc/Mod			ICD-10-CM		
	1	________		1	________
	2	________		2	________
	3	________		3	________
	4	________		4	________

24. Phyllis Young, age 41, had been hospitalized for a day when her doctor asked Dr. Samuel Sterns, a surgeon, to see her for abdominal pain. Dr. Sterns examined her and diagnosed gallstones. He scheduled Ms. Young for a laparoscopic cholecystectomy later that day.

Proc/Mod			ICD-10-CM		
	1	________		1	________
	2	________		2	________
	3	________		3	________
	4	________		4	________

Name ______________________

25. A mother brought her 6-month-old infant to the office for a trivalent split virus flu immunization and was seen by the nurse. The nurse reviewed the vaccine information sheet with the mother and gave her a copy of the document. The mother stated that she noticed that her son had a cough but there had been no change in his behavior and he did not act as though he were ill. He had no fever. The nurse checked and documented the child's vital signs and noted that there were no contraindications to administering the vaccine at today's visit.

Proc/Mod			ICD-10-CM		
	1	________		1	________
	2	________		2	________
	3	________		3	________
	4	________		4	________

Putting It All Together—Answers and Rationales

1. Proc/Mod: 1) 65710 Diagnosis: 1) H18.622

   The CPT code is in the eye section. Keratoconus is listed as stable (a slow, persistent worsening), acute (sudden, severe onset), or unstable. Since a "moderately progressive" disease state is not in the list, code the diagnosis as unstable.

2. Proc/Mod: 1) 99305, 2) 90875 Diagnosis: 1) F84.5, 2) F84.5

   CPT states that medical psychotherapy, when performed, is reported in addition to the E/M service.

3. Proc/Mod: 1) 99304 Diagnosis: 1) I63.9, 2) I69.344

   The physician's documentation supports an E/M code of 99304. The nursing facility will provide rehabilitation for the patient's residual monoplegia.

4. Proc/Mod: 1) 27130 Diagnosis: 1) M16.11

   This is a straightforward example of a surgical billing. There is no medical care reported by the surgeon as all related medical care is included in the surgical procedure.

5. Proc/Mod: 1) 90202-25, 2) 73120-LT, 3) 29280-FA, 4) A6449 q=1 Diagnosis: 1-4) S63.682A

   The modifier –25 would allow payment of the new patient office visit when a treatment is performed at the same visit. When reporting strapping, remember to include the required supplies. In this case, a fracture was not confirmed. Note that ICD-10-CM has specific codes for a sprain of the left thumb.

6. Proc/Mod: 1) 99235 Diagnosis: 1) H25.011, I49.9

   Procedure code 99235, rather than 99219, is correct because Dr. Black admitted and discharged (by a transfer of care) Mr. Brown on the same day. Dr. Green will report the initial hospital care service, 99221-99223. The diagnosis codes for Dr. Black would be the cataract first and arrhythmia second. "When a patient presents for outpatient surgery and develops complications requiring admission to observation, code the reason for the surgery as the first reported diagnosis (reason for the encounter) followed by codes for the complications as secondary diagnoses." (Guidelines, Section IV, A 2)

7. Proc/Mod: 1) 27500, 2) 21450-51-RT, 3) 26600-51-F8 Diagnosis: 1) S72.301A, 2) S02.609A, 3) S62.304A

Remember to put the most significant surgery on the first line, regardless of how they are listed on the operative note. Since the descriptions did not refer to a manipulation, use codes that state "no manipulation." Modifier –51 is required on the second and third services as well as the modifier describing the finger. Mandible diagnosis code will be "unspecified" since the part was not identified; the metacarpal and the shaft of the femur are identified and coded by site.

8. Proc/Mod: 1) 99238, 2) 94640, 3) J7613, 4) 99221-25 Diagnosis: 1) J45.902, 2) R06.2, 3) R06.2, 4) J45.901

This is an example of claims you will need to monitor. There are three claims: one for each hospitalization and one for the office services. The office visit is not billed as those services are related to the hospital admission of the same day. Modifier –25 is required for the admission as it is not related to the other E/M services (discharge and office visit) reported that day. The diagnosis for the discharge service, J45.902, describes the findings of her hospital stay. The diagnosis for the office services would be the symptom, wheezing, R06.2; the diagnosis for admission, J45.901, is asthma with acute exacerbation. Be prepared to fight for payment on this one.

9. Proc/Mod: 1) 99212, 2) 98926 Diagnosis: 1) J40 2) M99.09

Do not count on the fact there are two diagnoses to explain that the services are unrelated. Note the body regions identified in the CPT OMT codes. The diagnosis J40, bronchitis, is not specified as acute or chronic. The somatic dysfunction codes would be M99.09 as that code states abdomen and other; it is the diagnosis code for the OMT service, 98926.

10. Proc/Mod: 1) 99215, 2) 82948, 3) 82948-91 Diagnosis: 1) E11.649

The extended office visit is based on time, not the level of the examination. The repeat lab test in the office needs the –91 modifier. The metabolic panel was ordered, not performed in the office. The osteoarthritis was not treated on this visit, so the code is not included. The symptoms of uncoordinated and confused relate to the diagnosis of diabetes with hypoglycemia; therefore, would not be assigned as separate codes.

11. Proc/Mod: 1) 99231 Diagnosis: 1) N39.0, M54.9

A higher level of inpatient visit would be incorrect. The patient is probably stable today if he is to be discharged tomorrow. Today's complaint, backache, would be the diagnosis for this visit and the urinary tract infection would be reported as the diagnosis for the lab work ordered.

12. Proc/Mod: 1) 99213-25, 2) 93000-51, 3) 93015 Diagnosis: 1) I11.9, 2) R94.31, 3) R94.39

The office visit is likely to be an expanded problem focused visit with –25 to indicate the visit should not be included in the diagnostic tests. The 12-lead EKG could require the modifier –51 (or –59) or payers might bundle it in with the stress test. The diagnosis I11.9 would be used for the office visit; the EKG code is R94.31 while the best diagnosis for the stress test is the abnormal other cardiovascular test, R94.39. Avoid the diagnosis "ischemia" as the cause has not been determined based on the information available.

13. Proc/Mod: 1) 99215-25, 2) 95130 Diagnosis: 1) T63.441A 2) T63.441A

This is a problem of high severity. Modifier –25 should be used to indicate the office visit was separate from the injection. The same diagnosis can be reported for both services. Note that the ICD-10-CM code assumes the sting was unintentional as most people who are allergic to bees try to avoid them.

14. Proc/Mod: 1) 67938-54-RT, 2) 12011-54-51 Diagnosis: 1) S01.411A, 2) S01.121A, W33.01xA

Since the removal of an embedded foreign body is the major procedure, it should be reported first. Use modifier –54 on both procedures to indicate the services are surgical care only. The services relate to only one area of the body, so there probably would be no E/M service. Use diagnosis codes as appropriate for each site. If the documentation supported an E/M service, such as abrasions from other pieces of shot, it would be 99281-25, indicating it is unrelated to the surgical service. The gunshot accident code, W33.01xA, may be optional but since it was a gunshot wound it should be reported. Note that the "A" on each diagnosis code indicates this was the initial service.

15. Proc/Mod: 1) 99201-25, 2) 73070-LT, 3) 69210-50 Diagnosis: 1-2) S50.02xA, 3) H61.23

The examination was focused on the elbow and requires modifier –25 separate from the surgical service, 69210. Use modifier –LT on the x-ray. Get into the habit of using right and left indicators as laterality is significant in ICD-10-CM. Since there was no fracture or open wound, the diagnosis must be contusion for the first two services. The "A" indicates this is the first service for that diagnosis. CPT 2014 states to use modifier –50 if cerumen is removed from both ears, but some payers may not allow the –50 modifier so watch this claim carefully. You may need to rebill that service without the –50 modifier.

16. Dr. Brady's Proc/Mod: 1) 99460 q=1 Diagnosis: 1) Z00.110

Dr. Lewis's Proc/Mod: 1) 99223 Diagnosis: 1) P22.9

Dr. Brady's service was the newborn exam and is billable since he is not in practice with the neonatologist. The diagnosis, at the time of his visit, would have been a normal newborn. The problem occurred later. This was not stated as a "critical" admission, so the regular initial care services would be reported, but it would be reasonable to report a high level of service. Note the infant age range in ICD-10-CM. The "respiratory distress" should be coded in general terms only since it was not described as a syndrome.

17. Proc/Mod: 1) 90837, 2) 90901-51 Diagnosis: 1) F43.10, 2) F17.200

Use the two codes rather than any code that combines the two services into one code as they did not occur concurrently. Modifier –51 (or –59) clarifies two separate services. The diagnosis could be reported as PTSD (F43.10) for both services and nicotine dependence (F17.200) for the biofeedback. Avoid using codes from psychological trauma or psychosocial circumstances. For mental health services, it is advisable to code on the "light" side. Reveal no more than necessary to get the claim paid.

18. Proc/Mod: 1) 99213 Diagnosis: 1) E11.9

Assuming that she was the doctor who prescribed the meds six months ago, this would be an established patient visit. If Mr. Taylor is transferring to her practice and had no professional services in the past three years from Dr. Franklin or another physician of the same specialty in her former practice, this would be a new patient visit, 99202. The change in tax identification numbers and establishing a new chart does not make this a new patient visit. E11.9 will probably be one of the most used codes in ICD-10-CM.

19. Proc/Mod: 1) 10061-F7-TA Diagnosis: 1) L02.511, L72.3

Do not report two codes, 10060-F7 and 10060-TA (unless instructed to do so by the payer) as the description for 10061 states "multiple." Code 10061 would be the correct procedure code even though the treatment areas are separate. Report both diagnoses; the order of the diagnosis codes would not matter. Using both modifiers and two diagnosis codes may result in an adequate payment, but if it doesn't, that reporting could help with the appeal.

20. Proc/Mod: 1) 45333 Diagnosis: 1) D12.6

CPT states: "surgical endoscopy always includes diagnostic endoscopy." Code 45333 is used once regardless of the number of polyps removed. Also, it makes no difference if the polyp is removed whole or in pieces. The diagnosis should be polyp of the colon rather than rectal bleeding. As there is no mention of malignancy, be certain you select diagnosis codes from the benign section.

21. Proc/Mod: 1) 29881-RT, 2) G0289-51-RT Diagnosis: 1) S83.241A, 2) M93.961

The arthroscopic meniscectomy with chondroplasty is the major procedure and should be reported first. CMS created G0289 for reporting chondroplasty on a separate compartment. Modifier –51 would be reported first as it is a pricing modifier; modifier –RT explains that only the right knee was involved in the surgery. If you work for an orthopedic surgeon, contact the payers to determine if they will accept and pay for the G-code and if they allow it to be reported with a quantity of more than 1. Without documentation of old or current injury, the default in ICD-10-CM is current injury (S83.241A). Report S83.241A for the first service and osteochondritis M93.961 for the other service.

22. Proc/Mod: 1) 59821 Diagnosis: 1) O02.1

Note that the procedure code includes all the visits associated with the abortion and D&C service.

23. Proc/Mod: 1) 99213-25, 2) 11200 Diagnosis: 1) L57.0, 2) L91.8

The visit was more complex than the usual preoperative evaluation and postoperative care for a single skin tag with the finding of actinic keratoses. Modifier –25 is required for the office visit as 99213 was when the irritated skin tag was found. Use codes L57.0 for the office visit, and L91.8 for the surgical service.

24. Proc/Mod: 1) 99252-57, 2) 47562 Diagnosis: 1-2) K80.20

Dr. Sterns's first visit with the patient was the consultation, and the modifier –57 indicates that the decision for surgery was made then. The diagnosis is the same for both services. If Dr. Sterns wasn't certain it was gallstones, the doctor would not have scheduled surgery for later that day. However, if this lady had Medicare, CMS states this is not a consultation but should be reported as an initial or subsequent visit. Since the admitting physician (the primary care doctor) reported the initial day of inpatient care (yesterday), Dr. Sterns would report a subsequent hospital visit, 99231 or 99232, with the modifier –57. If this Medicare rule becomes part of a future CPT, this rule would apply to all payers.

25. Proc/Mod: 1) 99211-25, 2) 90657, 3) 90471 Diagnosis: 1) R05, 2-3) Z23

This is a good example of the proper use of code 99211 and the "cough" diagnosis for the visit. Had the child been examined yesterday and returned today for the immunization, you would report only the immunization (90657) and the administration service (90471).

EXAM QUESTIONS FOR CPT, CPT AND HCPCS, AND ICD-10-CM

Directions:

- Use the appropriate coding manual to determine the correct choice for each situation.
- Answer sheet is provided at the end of each exam for recording your choice for each question.

Name ___________________________

Exam Questions for CPT

Directions: Use the appropriate coding manual to determine the correct choice for each situation.

1. John underwent nerve grafting of the right foot, 3 cm.

   ① 64885-RT

   ② 64890-RT

   ③ 64891-RT

   ④ 64901-RT

2. Frank underwent thyroidectomy for removal of remaining thyroid tissue after previous right lobectomy for suspected malignancy.

   ① 60225

   ② 60240

   ③ 60260

   ④ 60270

3. Lucy, a nursing facility resident, was seen for annual assessment. What category of code(s) would be referenced for selecting a code?

   ① 99315–99316

   ② 99307–99310

   ③ 99318

   ④ 99339–33340

4. An 81-year-old patient receives anesthesia prior to undergoing cardioversion for persistent infrequent arrhythmia. Include physical status modifier with code.

   ① 00400-P2 + 99100

   ② 00410-P3 + 99140

   ③ 00410-P2 + 99100

   ④ 00410-P4 + 99100

5. Surgeon performs a sphenoid sinusotomy for removal of polyps, including biopsy.

   ① 31020

   ② 31050

   ③ 31051

   ④ 31070

6. Physician performs a surgical ligation of the common carotid artery.

   ① 37600

   ② 37605

   ③ 37606

   ④ 37615

7. A 67-year-old patient underwent contact laser vaporization of the prostate.

   ① 52450

   ② 52601

   ③ 52647

   ④ 52648

8. Mary underwent total abdominal hysterectomy, sparing the tubes and ovaries.

   ① 58150

   ② 58152

   ③ 58200

   ④ 58210

9. Radiologist directs and interprets the placement of a long gastrostomy tube in a patient who is status post cerebrovascular accident.

   ① 43246-26

   ② 74340

   ③ 74355

   ④ 74363

10. A nursing home patient was admitted for management of pneumonia, which is now resolved. The physician came by the facility to discharge the patient home, spending 20 minutes with the patient and family.

① 99217

② 99238

③ 99315

④ 99339

11. The physician conducted an initial office consultation for a 44-year-old patient, 6 years status post lumbar laminectomy with intractable sciatic pain, depression, and history of narcotic dependency or abuse. The physician performs a comprehensive history and examination with medical decision making of high complexity.

① 99241

② 99243

③ 99244

④ 99245

12. A 16-year-old patient undergoes excision of an aneurysmal bone cyst of the proximal right humerus, with allograft.

① 23155

② 23156

③ 23184

④ 23220

13. A 15-year-old, otherwise healthy patient receives anesthesia for electroconvulsive therapy. Include physical status modifier with code.

① 00104-P1

② 00104-P2

③ 00190-P1

④ 00210-P1

14. Robert, who is status post cochlear implant, has a visit for group rehabilitation, treatment of speech, and a processing disorder.

① 92507

② 92508

③ 92520

④ 92557

15. Health care employee receives the first of three hepatitis B vaccinations IM from her doctor.

① 90371 + 96372

② 90746 + 90471

③ 90746 + 96372

④ 96372

16. Janet underwent cervical conization with loop electrical excision of the transitional zone.

① 57460

② 57500

③ 57520

④ 57522

17. Mark had a stereotactic biopsy of intracranial lesion under MR guidance.

① 61720

② 61750

③ 61751

④ 61770

18. Dr. Harris counsels a group of teenagers regarding sexually transmitted diseases and prevention. Session lasts 30 minutes.

① 99401

② 99402

③ 99411

④ 99411-26

19. Dr. Nuri examines an 18-year-old in the emergency department for recurrent, severe menstrual migraine headache. The physician performs a problem-focused history and examination with straight-forward decision making.

① 99241

② 99281

③ 99282

④ 99284

20. Brian had an in-office simple incision and drainage of a pilonidal cyst.

① 10060

② 10061

③ 10080

④ 10081

21. Surgeon removes a Harrington rod in a patient with chronic irritation in the region of insertion.

① 22849

② 22850

③ 22852

④ 22899

22. Clyde, a patient with a congenital cleft palate, underwent a rhinoplasty with columellar lengthening, including the septum and tip.

① 30410

② 30430

③ 30460

④ 30462

23. A 34-year-old patient suspected of having sleep apnea had a sleep study with recording of ventilation, respiratory effort, heart rate, and oxygen saturation. A technologist was in attendance.

① 95805

② 95806

③ 95807

④ 95811

24. Surgeon performed excision of pterygium with grafting, left eye.

① 65400

② 65420-LT

③ 65426-LT

④ 66999

25. The neonatologist was asked to be on standby for 35 minutes for cesarean delivery of a baby in distress.

① 99360

② 99360 + 99360

③ 99464

④ 99465

26. Physician performed complex repair of a 3.2 cm scalp laceration.

① 13120

② 13120 + 13122

③ 13121

④ 13132

27. A 65-year-old patient receives anesthesia for repair of inguinal hernia. The patient has controlled hypertension. Include physical status modifier with code.

① 00830-P1

② 00830-P2

③ 00832-P1

④ 00832-P2

28. Leon underwent several burr holes in his skull with evacuation of subdural hematoma.

① 61105

② 61140

③ 61154

④ 61156

29. A 5-year-old patient, status post eardrum rupture, undergoes tympanic membrane repair with patch.

① 69433

② 69610

③ 69620

④ 69631

30. David was scheduled to see Dr. Bronson for his 6-month checkup and to have lab work done two weeks before his appointment on the 15th. As directed, the lab work was done on the first of the month. David called Dr. Bronson's office on the 3rd and talked to Dr. Bronson for 15 minutes about the tests. The doctor ordered two more tests done by the 5th so that the findings would be in the office for David's appointment on the 15th. What code would be reported for the service on the 3rd of the month?

① 99441

② 99442

③ 99443

④ 99444

31. Anesthesia was administered to Kelli for a gastric bypass procedure due to her morbid obesity. Include the physical status modifier with code.

① 00700-P3

② 00790-P2

③ 00790-P3

④ 00797-P3

32. Physician performed excision of inguinal hidradenitis with complex repair.

① 11450

② 11451

③ 11462

④ 11463

33. Rita was scheduled to undergo extensive internal and external hemorrhoidectomy with fistulectomy. Ten minutes prior to the start of the procedure, after anesthesia had been administered, she experienced a rapid decrease in heart rate, and the physician canceled the procedure. The physician would report which of the following codes?

① 46260 + 46261

② 46260-52

③ 46260-53

④ 46262-53

34. Luther underwent cystourethroscopy and laser ablation of two bladder tumors, each approximately 2.7 cm in size.

① 52204

② 52214

③ 52234

④ 52235

35. Anthony had an excision of Peyronie plaque with a 4.0 cm graft.

① 54060

② 54065

③ 54110

④ 54111

36. Hand specialist performs neuroplasty of the ulnar nerve of the left wrist.

① 64704-LT

② 64718-LT

③ 64719-LT

④ 64721-LT

37. Mason, age 15, is seen by his new doctor for a comprehensive physical examination and immunizations. He also has moderate acne on face and chest.

① 99384

② 99384-25

③ 99394

④ 99394-25

38. Arnold had his right thumb replanted following a complete amputation from the distal tip to the MP joint.

① 20816

② 20822

③ 20824

④ 20827

39. Curtis underwent operative laryngoscopy for removal of a chicken bone fragment.

① 31511

② 31530

③ 31531

④ 31577

40. Keith, who has a history of hypertriglyceridemia but with normal cholesterol, now has his triglyceride level determined.

① 82465

② 83718

③ 84478

④ 84485

41. A patient with asthma is evaluated for use of a nebulizer.

① 94640

② 94645

③ 94660

④ 94664

42. Dr. Ladwig performs an independent medical examination for patient Mr. Smith to determine Worker's Compensation impairment rating.

① 99450

② 99455

③ 99456

④ 99499

43. Joseph receives anesthesia for extracorporeal shock-wave lithotripsy with water bath. He has mild asthma. Include the physical status modifier with code.

① 00872-P1

② 00872-P2

③ 00873-P1

④ 00873-P2

44. Dr. Brush does a single-lung transplant with cardiopulmonary bypass employed during the procedure.

① 32851

② 32852

③ 32853

④ 32854

45. Sam has an intestinal intussusception and undergoes a reduction via laparotomy.

① 44005

② 44020

③ 44050

④ 44055

46. For Shirley's morbid obesity, a surgeon performs gastric bypass procedure with small intestine reconstruction to limit absorption.

① 43842

② 43846

③ 43847

④ 43848

47. Ms. Jones was seen in an initial office orthopedic consultation for bilateral trochanteric bursitis; her visit was considered problem-focused only.

① 99201

② 99241

③ 99242

④ 99251

48. Dr. Wilson repairs an abdominal aortic aneurysm caused by high-grade atherosclerosis.

① 35001

② 35081

③ 35082

④ 35091

49. Dr. Kelly successfully performed resuscitation for an infant suffering cardiac distress during delivery.

① 99461

② 99463

③ 99464

④ 99465

50. Helen underwent excision of a 1.5 cm malignant skin lesion of the left calf as well as removal of Norplant contraceptive capsules.

① 11402 + 11976

② 11602 + 11976

③ 11976 + 11622

④ 11983 + 11602

51. Bill returned to the office for a trigger point injection involving the trapezius and latissimus muscle groups.

① 20551

② 20552

③ 64415

④ 64420

52. Mr. Johnson underwent hepatic artery ligation with complex suture repair of a liver laceration from a motor vehicle accident.

① 47350

② 47360

③ 47360-51

④ 47361

53. Hospital follow-up visit by Dr. Stephens to see a 59-year-old female patient, status post uncomplicated left hip fixation. The physician performed a problem-focused history and physical examination with moderate decision making.

① 99221

② 99223

③ 99231

④ 99232

54. Family practitioner performed excision of a lipoma of the right forearm, 1.5 cm in diameter, followed by a simple wound closure.

① 11402

② 11402 + 12001

③ 11422

④ 11422 + 12031

55. Donor undergoes bone marrow harvesting for allogenic transplantation.

① 38220

② 38230

③ 38240

④ 38241

56. Sue had a total gastrectomy with Roux-en-Y reconstruction for stomach carcinoma.

① 43620

② 43621

③ 43631

④ 43633

57. Surgeon performed a simple Burch urethropexy on a 45-year-old patient.

① 51800

② 51840

③ 51841

④ 51992

58. A newly diagnosed patient with testicular cancer underwent radical orchiectomy with abdominal exploration via inguinal approach.

① 54520

② 54522

③ 54530

④ 54535

59. Ryan had a reconstruction of the mandibular rami due to blunt trauma, undergoing C osteotomy with bone graft.

① 21188

② 21193

③ 21194

④ 21195

60. A radiologist performed bilateral lymphangiography of the lower extremities, S&I (supervision and interpretation).

① 75801-26

② 75803-26

③ 75805-26

④ 75807-26

61. Marian was seen on an initial, comprehensive endocrinology office visit, having been referred for signs and symptoms of new-onset diabetes.

① 99201

② 99204

③ 99212

④ 99214

62. Terry underwent emergency laparoscopic appendectomy.

① 44950

② 44960

③ 44970

④ 44979

63. Rodney underwent nephrolithotomy for removal of a large staghorn calculus occupying the renal pelvis and calyces.

① 50060

② 50065

③ 50075

④ 50081

64. Harold had a flexible sigmoidoscopy with removal of two small polyps using snare technique.

① 45330

② 45333

③ 45338

④ 45339

65. Dr. Roberts conducts a home visit for a nonambulatory patient with progressive multiple sclerosis, now experiencing respiratory difficulty. The physician spent a total of 45 minutes with the new patient and family discussing treatment options and possible admission to a nursing facility. The physician performed a detailed history and exam with decision making of moderate complexity.

① 99342

② 99343

③ 99348

④ 99349

66. Dr. Peck performed a limited thoracotomy for a left lung mass.

① 32096

② 32097

③ 32035

④ 32551

67. Virginia underwent marsupialization of a Bartholin gland cyst.

① 10040

② 10060

③ 56420

④ 56440

68. Cathy received 15 minutes of ultrasound therapy on the left hip for bursitis.

① 97033

② 97035

③ 97110

④ 97124

69. Dorothy had symptoms of poisoning and underwent testing for the presence of arsenic.

① 82157

② 82175

③ 83015

④ 83018

70. Dolores underwent pericardial window creation for drainage of excess pericardial fluid.

① 33010

② 33015

③ 33020

④ 33025

71. Kurt has a simple papilloma of the penis and underwent cryosurgical removal.

① 54056

② 54057

③ 54065

④ 54110

72. Pain specialist physician performs single lumbar epidural steroid injection.

① 62280

② 62282

③ 62311

④ 62319

73. Joel had an emergency head CT scan without contrast following blunt trauma to the skull.

① 70450

② 70470

③ 70496

④ 70540

74. Nuclear medicine ventilation and perfusion lung scan was performed on a patient with sudden shortness of breath; aerosol technique was used, and two projections were obtained.

① 78579

② 78580

③ 78582

④ 78598

75. Ronald was treated with femoral-popliteal venous bypass grafting for severe occlusive disease.

① 35450

② 35521

③ 35556

④ 35566

76. Twelve-year-old Jane underwent dilation of the urethra under general anesthesia.

① 53605

② 53660

③ 53661

④ 53665

77. Emily had a radial keratotomy procedure in her right eye.

① 65710-RT

② 65760-RT

③ 65767-RT

④ 65771-RT

78. Combative patient underwent removal of burrowed insect from external auditory canal; general anesthesia was required.

① 69145

② 69200

③ 69205

④ 69220

79. Lana, an expectant mother of twins in her second trimester, underwent obstetrical ultrasound with a fetal anatomic exam.

① 76805 + 76810

② 76811 + 76812

③ 76815

④ 76856

80. The lab performs a test to determine the therapeutic level for a patient taking lithium.

① 80101

② 80102

③ 80176

④ 80178

81. A steelworker was seen in the emergency room for acute eye pain associated with a probable steel shaving in the eye; none was found. The physician performed a problem-focused history and physician examination with straight-forward decision making.

① 99281

② 99283

③ 99284

④ 99285

82. Dr. Bale performs a closure of a rectovaginal fistula by vaginal approach.

① 57284

② 57300

③ 57305

④ 57310

83. Lucas underwent before-and-after contrast MRI studies of the pelvis.

① 72191

② 72193

③ 72197

④ 72198

84. Dr. Hall performed an open repair of a femoral neck fracture with internal fixation.

① 27230

② 27235

③ 27236

④ 27244

85. Susan underwent tubal occlusion with the use of Falope rings, vaginal approach.

① 58600

② 58615

③ 58671

④ 58700

86. Marshall receives a chiropractic manipulative treatment for pain in the temporomandibular joint region.

① 97140

② 98925

③ 98940

④ 98943

87. Bruce undergoes a sex-change operation from male to female.

① 55899

② 55970

③ 55980

④ 58999

88. The pregnant patient was visiting out-of-town family members when she went into labor. She returned home after delivery. The physician that delivers the infant would report which of the following codes?

① 59400

② 59409

③ 59610

④ 59620

89. Margaret underwent a right cataract extraction with the insertion of an intraocular lens via phacoemulsification technique.

① 66830

② 66850

③ 66982

④ 66984

90. The CPT Category III codes are updated quarterly.

① True

② False

91. The doctor orders a urinalysis to screen for bacteria.

① 81000

② 81002

③ 81003

④ 81007

92. Lillian has an automated CBC, WBC, and platelet count.

① 85025

② 85027

③ 85041

④ 85048

93. Dr. Roberts orders a test for total hepatitis A antibodies.

① 86706

② 86707

③ 86708

④ 86709

94. May underwent debridement with dressing for a small epidermal burn of the forearm in Dr. Gray's office.

① 16000

② 16020

③ 16025

④ 16030

95. Martin underwent magnetic resonance imaging of the chest, with before-and-after contrast studies, to rule out a mass.

① 71550

② 71551

③ 71552

④ 71555

96. Mary Johnson had a closed manipulation of her distal fibular fracture.

① 27781

② 27786

③ 27788

④ 27792

97. The surgeon performs a laparoscopic-assisted vaginal hysterectomy (uterus 240 g) with bilateral salpingo-oophorectomy.

① 58260 + 58720

② 58262

③ 58552

④ 58552 + 58720

98. Grant is hospitalized for a mobilization rearrangement repair of a conjunctival laceration.

① 65270

② 65272

③ 65273

④ 65285

99. The operative note states Gordon underwent excision of a lesion of the mucosa and underlying muscle of the vestibule of the mouth.

① 40812

② 40814

③ 40816

④ 40820

100. Dr. Jones performed a biopsy of the left breast, using a localization wire, under ultrasound guidance.

① 19081

② 19083

③ 19085

④ 19125

Name ___________________________

Answers to Exam Questions: CPT

1. ① ② ③ ④	30. ① ② ③ ④	59. ① ② ③ ④	88. ① ② ③ ④
2. ① ② ③ ④	31. ① ② ③ ④	60. ① ② ③ ④	89. ① ② ③ ④
3. ① ② ③ ④	32. ① ② ③ ④	61. ① ② ③ ④	90. ① ②
4. ① ② ③ ④	33. ① ② ③ ④	62. ① ② ③ ④	91. ① ② ③ ④
5. ① ② ③ ④	34. ① ② ③ ④	63. ① ② ③ ④	92. ① ② ③ ④
6. ① ② ③ ④	35. ① ② ③ ④	64. ① ② ③ ④	93. ① ② ③ ④
7. ① ② ③ ④	36. ① ② ③ ④	65. ① ② ③ ④	94. ① ② ③ ④
8. ① ② ③ ④	37. ① ② ③ ④	66. ① ② ③ ④	95. ① ② ③ ④
9. ① ② ③ ④	38. ① ② ③ ④	67. ① ② ③ ④	96. ① ② ③ ④
10. ① ② ③ ④	39. ① ② ③ ④	68. ① ② ③ ④	97. ① ② ③ ④
11. ① ② ③ ④	40. ① ② ③ ④	69. ① ② ③ ④	98. ① ② ③ ④
12. ① ② ③ ④	41. ① ② ③ ④	70. ① ② ③ ④	99. ① ② ③ ④
13. ① ② ③ ④	42. ① ② ③ ④	71. ① ② ③ ④	100. ① ② ③ ④
14. ① ② ③ ④	43. ① ② ③ ④	72. ① ② ③ ④	
15. ① ② ③ ④	44. ① ② ③ ④	73. ① ② ③ ④	
16. ① ② ③ ④	45. ① ② ③ ④	74. ① ② ③ ④	
17. ① ② ③ ④	46. ① ② ③ ④	75. ① ② ③ ④	
18. ① ② ③ ④	47. ① ② ③ ④	76. ① ② ③ ④	
19. ① ② ③ ④	48. ① ② ③ ④	77. ① ② ③ ④	
20. ① ② ③ ④	49. ① ② ③ ④	78. ① ② ③ ④	
21. ① ② ③ ④	50. ① ② ③ ④	79. ① ② ③ ④	
22. ① ② ③ ④	51. ① ② ③ ④	80. ① ② ③ ④	
23. ① ② ③ ④	52. ① ② ③ ④	81. ① ② ③ ④	
24. ① ② ③ ④	53. ① ② ③ ④	82. ① ② ③ ④	
25. ① ② ③ ④	54. ① ② ③ ④	83. ① ② ③ ④	
26. ① ② ③ ④	55. ① ② ③ ④	84. ① ② ③ ④	
27. ① ② ③ ④	56. ① ② ③ ④	85. ① ② ③ ④	
28. ① ② ③ ④	57. ① ② ③ ④	86. ① ② ③ ④	
29. ① ② ③ ④	58. ① ② ③ ④	87. ① ② ③ ④	

Name ______________________

Exam Questions for CPT and HCPCS

Directions: Use the appropriate coding manual to determine the correct choice for each situation.

1. To report ambulance services for a Medicare patient ordered by a physician, use modifier:

   ① -QM

   ② -QN

   ③ -RC

   ④ -RT

2. Luke underwent simple incision and drainage of an abscess on his thigh. The wound was packed with iodoform gauze (approximately 2 × 2). Select the correct codes for the procedure and the gauze.

   ① 10060 + A6220

   ② 10060 + A6222

   ③ 10061 + A6222

   ④ 10061 + A6223

3. HCPCS Level II codes are four-position alphanumeric codes used to represent items not included in Level I (CPT) codes.

   ① True

   ② False

4. Leo undergoes an IVP but has a severe reaction to the contrast material. The IVP procedure is discontinued. Which modifier is used to describe this situation?

   ① -22

   ② -52

   ③ -53

   ④ -56

5. Grace was seen in the urgent care center with signs and symptoms of dehydration. She was observed for 8 hours while receiving IV normal saline infusion, 1000 mL. Select the correct HCPCS code for the infusion.

   ① J7030

   ② J7040

   ③ J7050

   ④ J7120

6. The L group of codes represents which procedures or products?

   ① Pathology and laboratory

   ② Drugs and enterals

   ③ Orthotics and prosthetics

   ④ Speech and language services

7. In CPT coding, the history, examination, and medical decision making are considered the key components in selecting the level of E/M services.

   ① True

   ② False

8. If a patient has trigger thumb release performed on the right, which modifier is used for the anatomic location?

   ① -F4

   ② -F5

   ③ -F9

   ④ -FA

9. A nursing facility patient developed multiple decubitus ulcers during a hospital stay. Her physician readmitted her to the nursing facility, performed a detailed history and exam, developed a new plan of care, and ordered an air-fluidized bed for treatment. Select the correct E/M and HCPCS codes.

   ① 99304 + E0193

   ② 99304 + E0194

   ③ 99305 + E0193

   ④ 99305 + E0194

10. HCPCS Level II codes are maintained by the American Medical Association.

   ① True

   ② False

11. A patient was seen in consultation for possible surgery. The surgeon schedules the procedure for the following day. Which modifier would you choose to indicate the decision for surgery?

   ① -54

   ② -55

   ③ -56

   ④ -57

12. Select the correct HCPCS code for an insertion tray without drainage bag or catheter.

   ① A4310

   ② A4311

   ③ A4312

   ④ A4313

13. Select the correct HCPCS code for below-knee-length surgical stockings.

   ① A4490

   ② A4495

   ③ A4500

   ④ A4510

14. According to CPT definitions, a patient treated in an ambulatory facility would be classified as an outpatient.

   ① True

   ② False

15. John has incision and drainage of an abscess involving the left fourth toe. Identify the correct modifier.

   ① -T2

   ② -T3

   ③ -T6

   ④ -T8

16. Linda was seen in the office for a facial chemical peel, epidermal only.

   ① 15780

   ② 15786

   ③ 15788

   ④ 15789

17. H codes in HCPCS represent the official codes for durable medical equipment.

   ① True

   ② False

18. Dennis arrived in the emergency department with acute shortness of breath. During his observation in the emergency department, multiple arterial blood gas testing was performed to monitor his improvement. Which modifier would you choose to accurately code the multiple ABGs?

   ① -51

   ② -90

   ③ -91

   ④ -99

19. Select the correct HCPCS code for a tourniquet used by a dialysis patient.

① A4911

② A4913

③ A4918

④ A4929

20. Select the correct HCPCS code for a pair of aluminum underarm crutches.

① E0110

② E0112

③ E0114

④ E0116

21. Physical status modifiers in CPT are used to distinguish the varying levels of complexity of surgical services provided.

① True

② False

22. A Medicare patient received a wheelchair two months ago, but the beneficiary has not decided whether to purchase or rent. Which HCPCS modifier would you use?

① -BO

② -BP

③ -BR

④ -BU

23. A teenager, new to the practice, was seen in a problem-focused visit for symptoms of tonsillitis and pharyngitis. She was given an injection of azithromycin for her acute symptoms. Select the correct E/M and HCPCS codes.

① 99201 + J0290

② 99201 + J0456

③ 99202 + J0290

④ 99202 + J0456

24. It is acceptable to code HCPCS from index entries only.

① True

② False

25. A 31-year-old patient was seen by her family doctor for a routine physical exam. During the exam, the patient was noted to have high blood pressure. The physician discussed the new finding with the patient, and the patient disclosed she has been under a great deal of stress due to the demands of her work and impending divorce. The high blood pressure was deemed stress-related, and the physician and the patient discussed stress reduction techniques. As a result of the extended discussion with the patient, the visit was prolonged 35 minutes beyond the normally expected length for a routine physical exam. Which CPT code(s) or modifier(s) would you use to document the additional time spent with the patient?

① 99395-P3

② 99395-22

③ 99395 + 99354

④ 99358

26. Select the correct HCPCS code for a surgically implanted electrical osteogenesis stimulator.

① E0748

② E0749

③ E0760

④ E0761

27. Select the correct HCPCS code to report a patient receiving an injection of amphotericin B, 50 mg.

① J0285

② J0287 x5

③ J0288 x 5

④ J0289 x 5

28. The general definition of the CPT surgical package includes the patient's preoperative evaluation on the day of the procedure, the surgical procedure and its usual components, and the patient's uncomplicated follow-up care.

① True

② False

29. The patient had a skin tag removed from her upper right eyelid. Which HCPCS modifier identifies this location?

① -El

② -E2

③ -E3

④ -E4

30. An infant born with clubfoot on the right was seen in the pediatric orthopedic clinic as a new patient. The physician conducted a problem-focused history and examination and prescribed a clubfoot wedge for the patient. Select the correct codes for the visit and the wedge.

① 99201 + L3201

② 99201 + L3380

③ 99212 + L3201

④ 99212 + L3380

31. The HCPCS route of administration "JA" means the patient is receiving the drug intravenously.

① True

② False

32. The patient was seen in the office for exercise stress testing. When the physician was placing the EKG leads, she noticed a suspicious mole on the patient's chest and excised the lesion. What CPT modifier would you use to indicate the additional procedure performed during this E/M visit?

① -24

② -25

③ -51

④ -53

33. A patient was seen in the office for acute hives. The doctor gave her a 25 mg injection of hydroxyzine. Select the correct HCPCS code.

① J3400

② J3410

③ J3470

④ J3485

34. Select the correct HCPCS code for an orthopedic shoe insole made of felt and covered with leather.

① L3500

② L3520

③ L3540

④ L3570

35. To measure and code the removal of a lesion using CPT guidelines, the lesion size must be expressed in inches.

① True

② False

36. If a patient is prescribed oxygen therapy at 0.5 liters per minute, which HCPCS modifier describes this flow rate?

① -QE

② -QF

③ -QG

④ -QH

37. An established patient was seen in the office because of difficulty toileting after hip replacement surgery. Her family doctor examined her and sent her home with a stationary commode chair with fixed arms to use during her recovery period. The physician performed a problem-focused history and physical exam with straight-forward decision making. Select the appropriate codes.

① 99211 + E0163

② 99211 + E0165

③ 99212 + E0163

④ 99212 + E0165

38. All HCPCS codes and descriptions are updated monthly by CMS.

① True

② False

39. Which CPT modifier would you choose to indicate a patient received a service or procedure that was less than originally intended?

① -22

② -32

③ -51

④ -52

40. Select the correct HCPCS code that describes the reduction of an ocular prosthesis.

① V2623

② V2625

③ V2626

④ V2629

41. John received an intramuscular injection of 2 mg of Haldol in the physician's office. Select the correct HCPCS code.

① J1630

② J1631

③ J3410

④ J3470

42. When coding bilateral procedures in CPT, you must always list the code twice.

① True

② False

43. The mobile x-ray service came to the nursing facility to x-ray Mrs. Jones for possible hip fracture. The x-ray will be interpreted tomorrow by the radiologist. Which HCPCS modifier would you use for today's service?

① -TA

② -TC

③ -TD

④ -TE

44. A Medicare patient with diabetes saw the doctor for routine foot care: the cutting of three calluses and debridement of all 10 toenails.

① 11056 + 11719

② 11056 + 11721

③ 11057 + 11720

④ S0390

45. Laboratory services in HCPCS are listed in the P codes grouping.

① True

② False

46. Which CPT modifier would you use to indicate that an outside laboratory was used to process a patient's specimen?

① -56

② -90

③ -91

④ -99

47. Select the correct HCPCS code for a patient receiving nonemergency minibus transportation in a mountain area.

① A0080

② A0110

③ A0120

④ A0160

48. Some radiology procedures include two parts: a technical component and a professional component.

① True

② False

49. A patient has used his wheelchair for nearly four years. Due to wear, he now needs a replacement for the right footrest. Which HCPCS modifier is used to indicate this replacement?

① -RA

② -RB

③ -RR

④ -RT

50. Marvin was referred to the office of a wound care specialist for consultation regarding his nonhealing surgical wound. Dr. Bell spent approximately 30 minutes and performed an expanded problem-focused history and examination with straight-forward decision making. The patient was sent home on a topical hyperbaric oxygen chamber therapy for wound healing. Select the correct codes.

① 99241 + A4575

② 99242 + A4575

③ 99251 + A4575

④ 99252 + A4575

51. Drugs listed in HCPCS are identified by both brand and generic names.

① True

① False

52. Leon had an emergency cholecystectomy six days after having a lung biopsy. The same surgeon performed both procedures. Which CPT modifier is used on the second surgery?

① -58

② -59

③ -78

④ -79

53. What is the correct HCPCS code for a patient that requires gradient compression stockings, full length 30–40 mmHg?

① A6531

② A6534 x 2

③ A6537 x 2

④ A6540

54. Rose was seen for insertion of a temporary, indwelling latex Foley urinary catheter. Select the correct codes.

① 51701 + A4314

② 51701 + A4338

③ 51702 + A4338

④ 51703 + A4328

55. According to CPT coding guidelines, a pathology consultation includes a medical interpretive report.

① True

② False

56. Dr. Wilkins amputated Stanley's right lower extremity (BKA). His staff PA was the assistant during the procedure. Which HCPCS modifier would you choose to indicate the PA's role in this procedure?

① -AD

② -AM

③ -AS

④ -AT

57. Wilbur was seen by the nurse for a routine visit in the multiple sclerosis clinic. He received an injection of beta-1a interferon, 30 mcg, from the nurse in the clinic. Select the appropriate codes.

① 99211 + J1826

② 99211 + J9212

③ 99212 + J1826

④ 99212 + J9214

58. HCPCS ambulance modifiers always include one alpha character and one numeric character.

① True

② False

59. Anesthesia is administered, and the physician begins to perform a diagnostic flexible fiberoptic laryngoscopy. Due to equipment failure, the procedure could not be accomplished. Which of the following would be used to report the physician's services?

① 31505-52

② 31525-52

③ 31525-53

④ 31575-53

60. Select the correct HCPCS code for a drainable rubber ostomy pouch with a faceplate attached.

① A4375

② A4376

③ A4377

④ A4378

61. Select the correct HCPCS code for replacement handgrip for a cane that the patient owns.

① A4635

② A4636

③ A4637

④ A4640

62. In CPT coding, when the patient receives an immune globulin product, you must also include an administration code as appropriate.

① True

② False

63. An ambulance was called to come to the aid of a choking patient; however, the patient expired before the ambulance arrived on the scene. Which HCPCS modifier would you use to document this circumstance?

① -QK

② -QL

③ -QM

④ -QP

64. Robin underwent unattended sleep study with monitoring of oxygen saturation and chest movement. He was not able to sleep adequately throughout the study, and the study was equivocal. He was provided with a recording apnea monitor for home use. Select the appropriate codes.

① 95806 + E0618

② 95806 + E0619

③ 95807 + E0618

④ 95807 + E0619

65. The two levels of national HCPCS codes can be applied to both inpatient and outpatient services by physicians.

① True

② False

66. Which CPT modifier is used to indicate a repeat procedure performed by a different physician?

① -58

② -76

③ -77

④ -78

67. Select the correct HCPCS code for a hydrogel dressing with an adhesive border used to cover a 24-square inch wound.

① A6242

② A6244

③ A6246

④ A6247

68. Select the correct HCPCS code for home mix parenteral nutritional additives, to include electrolytes.

① B4197

② B4199

③ B4216

④ B4220

69. When coding in CPT, no distinction is made between new and established patients in the emergency department.

① True

② False

70. Peggy was seen in the contraceptive clinic two weeks after delivery of her child. She was fitted with a copper intrauterine device. Select the codes for the fitting and the device.

① 58300 + J7303

② 58300 + J7300

③ 58301 + J7303

④ 58301 + J7300

71. Select the correct HCPCS code for a replacement brake attachment on a wheeled walker.

① E0143

② E0147

③ E0155

④ E0159

72. Select the correct HCPCS code for a patient admitted as an inpatient to a residential addiction program for acute alcohol detoxification.

① H0009

② H0011

③ H0012

④ H0013

73. Richard received a two-lead TENS unit for pain control after suffering a fractured radius. Select appropriate codes.

① 64550 + E0720

② 64550 + E0730

③ 64575 + E0720

④ 64575 + E0730

74. Select the correct HCPCS code for an injection of methylprednisolone acetate, 40 mg.

① J1020 x 2

② J1030

③ J1040

④ J2920

75. A patient came to the office to have a B12 level analysis and to receive her weekly B12 shot. Select the correct codes.

① 82607 + J3420

② 82607 + J3430

③ 82608 + J3420

④ 82608 + J3430

76. Select the HCPCS code that correctly identifies a unit of leukocyte-reduced platelets.

① P9019

② P9020

③ P9031

④ P9034

77. Select the correct HCPCS code for 1 mg of inhaled dexamethasone in concentrated form.

① J1094

② J1100

③ J7637

④ J7638

78. A patient who is status post left-sided CVA was seen for weight loss and other symptoms indicative of dysphagia. Speech pathology provides dysphagia screening and her first treatment for the swallowing dysfunction. Select the correct codes.

① 92526 + V5362

② 92526 + V5364

③ 92610 + V5362

④ 92610 + V5364

79. Select the correct HCPCS code for a nonheated humidifier used with a positive airway pressure device.

① A7039

② E0550

③ E0560

④ E0561

80. Dr. Hoyt spent 30 minutes with the patient and family to discuss discharge plans on the day of discharge as well as the patient's immediate at-home care. Paul had undergone his second below-knee amputation and was given a transfer board for use at home. Select the codes for the discharge visit and the transfer board.

① 99238 + E0705

② 99238 + E1035

③ 99239 + E0705

④ 99239 + E1035

81. Select the correct HCPCS code that reflects the supply of a one-dose vial of technetium Tc 99m disofenin.

① A9500

② A9502

③ A9510

④ A9536

82. Identify the HCPCS code that describes a full-leg, segmental pneumatic appliance with compressor.

① E0650

② E0660

③ E0667

④ E0671

83. Select the HCPCS code for an injection of 2 grams of cefotaxime sodium.

① J0694 x2

② J0696

③ J0697

④ J0698 x 2

84. To report the services of one CRNA directed by the anesthesiologist for the fifth concurrent procedure supervised by that physician, use modifier:

① -QS

② -QX

③ -QY

④ -QZ

85. To report the services of the anesthesiologist in question 84, use modifier:

① -AA

② -AD

③ -QK

④ -QY

86. At the physician's direction, the RN called the patient at home to monitor the patient's program for control of her severe arthritis.

① S0220

② S0271

③ S0315

④ S0320

87. John was fitted with a custom-made compression burn garment for severe burns of the chest and upper back.

① A6501

② A6509

③ A6510

④ A6511

88. A patient with a fractured femur and tibia had a trapeze and grab bar attached to a hospital bed in his home.

① E0910

② E0920

③ E0940

④ E0941

89. Five patients participated in the group psychotherapy session and received free educational materials.

① 90834 + 99071

② 90846 + 99070

③ 90853 + 99071

④ 90901 + 99070

90. A patient received a Blom Singer speech valve.

① L8499

② L8500

③ L8501

④ L8507

91. Tracy got a replacement for a lost gas-permeable bifocal contact lens.

① V2430

② V2502

③ V2512

④ V2522

92. What HCPCS code would be reported for a bilateral digital screening mammography?

① G0202

② G0202 x 2

③ G0204

④ G0206

93. A defined formula (100 calories to a unit) to meet a special metabolic need when administered through a feeding tube is reported with code:

① B4150

② B4152

③ B4153

④ B4154

94. Dr. Johnson serves a large rural area, and some patients request their E/M services via the Internet. These documented encounters would be reported with code:

① 99056

② 99347

③ 99441

④ 99444

95. The infant with a left club foot was treated by manipulation and a short leg cast.

① 29405-LT

② 29425-LT

③ 29450-LT

④ 29799-LT

96. Mary's mother and sister have known BRCA1 mutation, and she now undergoes testing for the mutation.

① 81206

② 81210

③ 81214

④ 81216

97. A store specializing in shoes for diabetic patients supplied a patient with a pair that had a metatarsal bar.

① A5500 x 2

② A5503 x 2

③ A5504 x 2

④ A5505 x 2

98. Following his hospitalization, Ken went home with cervical traction equipment that fits over a door.

① E0840

② E0850

③ E0860

④ E0870

99. The patient was authorized to receive a new 12-volt battery charger.

① L7360

② L7362

③ L7364

④ L7366

100. A patient received 1 g of Gammagard liquid immune globulin intravenously from the nurse in his doctor's office, 45 minutes.

① 90281 + J1460

② 90281 + J1559

③ 90471 + J1559

④ 96365 + J1569 x 2

Name ____________________

Answers to Exam Questions: CPT and HCPCS

1. ① ② ③ ④
2. ① ② ③ ④
3. ① ②
4. ① ② ③ ④
5. ① ② ③ ④
6. ① ② ③ ④
7. ① ②
8. ① ② ③ ④
9. ① ② ③ ④
10. ① ②
11. ① ② ③ ④
12. ① ② ③ ④
13. ① ② ③ ④
14. ① ②
15. ① ② ③ ④
16. ① ② ③ ④
17. ① ②
18. ① ② ③ ④
19. ① ② ③ ④
20. ① ② ③ ④
21. ① ②
22. ① ② ③ ④
23. ① ② ③ ④
24. ① ②
25. ① ② ③ ④
26. ① ② ③ ④
27. ① ② ③ ④
28. ① ②
29. ① ② ③ ④
30. ① ② ③ ④
31. ① ②
32. ① ② ③ ④
33. ① ② ③ ④
34. ① ② ③ ④
35. ① ②
36. ① ② ③ ④
37. ① ② ③ ④
38. ① ②
39. ① ② ③ ④
40. ① ② ③ ④
41. ① ② ③ ④
42. ① ②
43. ① ② ③ ④
44. ① ② ③ ④
45. ① ②
46. ① ② ③ ④
47. ① ② ③ ④
48. ① ②
49. ① ② ③ ④
50. ① ② ③ ④
51. ① ②
52. ① ② ③ ④
53. ① ② ③ ④
54. ① ② ③ ④
55. ① ②
56. ① ② ③ ④
57. ① ② ③ ④
58. ① ②
59. ① ② ③ ④
60. ① ② ③ ④
61. ① ② ③ ④
62. ① ②
63. ① ② ③ ④
64. ① ② ③ ④
65. ① ②
66. ① ② ③ ④
67. ① ② ③ ④
68. ① ② ③ ④
69. ① ②
70. ① ② ③ ④
71. ① ② ③ ④
72. ① ② ③ ④
73. ① ② ③ ④
74. ① ② ③ ④
75. ① ② ③ ④
76. ① ② ③ ④
77. ① ② ③ ④
78. ① ② ③ ④
79. ① ② ③ ④
80. ① ② ③ ④
81. ① ② ③ ④
82. ① ② ③ ④
83. ① ② ③ ④
84. ① ② ③ ④
85. ① ② ③ ④
86. ① ② ③ ④
87. ① ② ③ ④
88. ① ② ③ ④
89. ① ② ③ ④
90. ① ② ③ ④
91. ① ② ③ ④
92. ① ② ③ ④
93. ① ② ③ ④
94. ① ② ③ ④
95. ① ② ③ ④
96. ① ② ③ ④
97. ① ② ③ ④
98. ① ② ③ ④
99. ① ② ③ ④
100. ① ② ③ ④

Name ___________________

Exam Questions for ICD-10-CM

Directions: Use the appropriate coding manual to determine the correct choice for each situation.

1. A patient seen in the office today has known Graves' disease, now with signs and symptoms of a thyroid storm.

   ① E05.01

   ② E05.20

   ③ E05.90

   ④ E05.91

2. A 3-year-old patient was brought in by her mother because of fever, fussiness, and tugging at the right ear. Otoscopy confirmed acute infection with erythema and pus of the canal.

   ① H65.191

   ② H65.194

   ③ H66.001

   ④ H66.002

3. A patient was seen because of pain and swelling of the right elbow. The joint does not appear to be unstable, but there is effusion. Rule out fracture.

   ① M25.421

   ② M25.521

   ③ S42.391A

   ④ A42.401A

4. Robert took the ampicillin as directed but returns to the office today with urticaria and swelling, classic signs of allergic reaction.

   ① L50.0, T36.0x5A

   ② L50.8

   ③ L50.0, T36.0x4A

   ④ T88.6

5. Newly diagnosed asthma patient was counseled regarding asthma therapy and the correct use of a nebulizer.

   ① Z71.89

   ② Z71.9

   ③ Z97.8

   ④ Z99.89

6. The patient is brought to the physician's office for red sores. The physician documents the diagnosis as impetigo.

   ① L01.00

   ② L01.01

   ③ L01.09

   ④ R21

7. Thomas was seen for evaluation of pilonidal cyst.

   ① L05.01

   ② L05.02

   ③ L05.91

   ④ L05.92

8. John came to the office for examination of a penile lesion; his physician determined it to be a classic plaque of Peyronie's disease.

   ① N47.8

   ② N48.0

   ③ N48.6

   ④ N48.29

9. Betsy was seen for annual gynecological exam including Pap smear. Findings were normal.

   ① Z01.411, Z12.4

   ② Z01.411, Z12.72

   ③ Z01.419, Z12.4

   ④ Z01.419, Z12.72

10. Visit regarding patient needing a refill for her birth-control pills.

    ① Z30.40

    ② Z30.41

    ③ Z30.431

    ④ Z30.49

11. Brian suffered a dislocation of the left shoulder.

    ① S43.001A

    ② S43.004A

    ③ S43.005A

    ④ S43.006A

12. Select the correct code for a unilateral strangulated inguinal hernia.

    ① K40.30

    ② K40.31

    ③ K40.90

    ④ K40.91

13. Marie was seen for vaginal spotting in her 21st week of pregnancy.

    ① O26.851, Z3A.21

    ② O26.852, Z3A.21

    ③ O26.853, Z3A.21

    ④ O26.859, Z3A.21

14. A 35-year-old female was seen in the office today for evaluation of a breast lump.

    ① N61

    ② N62

    ③ N63

    ④ N64.5

15. A 16-year-old male was seen in the clinic for severe sore throat, redness, cough, and erythema. Rapid strep test was positive. The diagnosis is documented as *Streptococcal pharyngitis*.

    ① J02.0

    ② J02.8

    ③ J02.8, B95.5

    ④ J02.9

16. Select the correct code for personal history of cervical carcinoma.

    ① C53.9

    ② Z80.49

    ③ Z85.41

    ④ Z85.44

17. Adam was seen for treatment of acute posttraumatic stress disorder.

    ① F43.0

    ② F43.10

    ③ F43.11

    ④ F43.12

18. The patient was diagnosed with a chronic gastric ulcer with bleeding.

    ① K25.0

    ② K25.3

    ③ K25.4

    ④ K25.6

19. The physician documents the following diagnosis: alcoholic hepatitis with alcohol dependence and withdrawal delirium.

    ① F10.231, K70.10

    ② F10.239, K70.10

    ③ F10.230, K70.11

    ④ F10.231, K70.11

20. Abby was seen for a puncture wound of the right forearm.

① S41.131A

② S51.811A

③ S51.831A

④ S51.841A

21. Fred came to the office to discuss treatment options for a new diagnosis of malignant melanoma of the forehead.

① C43.30

② C43.39

③ C43.9

④ C44.309

22. Robin was brought in for evaluation of skin tags of the neck.

① L91.0

② L91.8

③ L91.9

④ L98.9

23. Mark's daughter brought her father in for follow-up of early-onset Alzheimer's dementia.

① G30.0, F02.80

② G30.0, F02.81

③ G30.8, F02.80

④ G30.9, F02.80

24. Karen was brought into the office for evaluation and examination after swallowing a dime.

① T17.208A

② T18.2xxA

③ T18.8xxA

④ T18.9xxA

25. A vacationing patient was seen in the urgent care clinic for second-degree sunburn of both shoulder areas.

① L55.0

② L55.1

③ L55.9

④ T22.251A, T22.252A

26. Select the correct code for chlamydial conjunctivitis.

① A74.0

② A74.89

③ A74.0, H10.9

④ H10.9

27. Ronda came into the office seeking treatment for a fungal toenail infection.

① B35.1

② L03.032

③ L08.9

④ L08.9, B49

28. Terry was seen in the office today for a routine follow-up after suffering a comminuted fracture of the shaft of the left femur. Physician notes that the fracture is healing.

① S72.352A

② S72.352D

③ S72.355A

④ S72.355D

29. Clifton was seen for removal of a Jackson-Pratt drain inserted last week after cholecystectomy.

① Z48.02

② Z48.03

③ Z48.817

④ Z51.89

30. Six-year-old Jason was brought in for additional testing for color blindness.

① H53.50

② H53.52

③ H53.59

④ H53.9

31. The patient was seen for complaints of increased urinary frequency due to benign prostatic hypertrophy.

① N40.0, R35.0

② N40.0

③ N40.1

④ N40.1, R35.0

32. Select the correct code(s) for malignant hypertensive heart disease with stage 3 chronic renal failure.

① I11.9, I12.9, N18.3

② I13.10, N18.9

③ I13.10, N18.9

④ I13.11, N18.3

33. Harold was seen for preoperative cardiovascular evaluation prior to undergoing cholecystectomy.

① Z01.810

② Z01.818

③ Z01.89

④ Z02.89

34. Joe was seen in the emergency department for a nondisplaced fracture of the trapezoid, smaller multiangular, of the right wrist.

① S62.174A

② S62.175A

③ S62.181A

④ S62.184A

35. Select the correct code(s) for cellulitis of the colostomy site.

① K94.00

② K94.02, L03.311

③ N99.511

④ T85.698A, L03.311

36. Select the correct code for Charcôt's joint of the right knee.

① M14.651

② M14.661

③ M14.671

④ M14.669

37. Helen was seen by the gastroenterologist for evaluation of prolapsed internal hemorrhoids and anal fissure.

① K64.1

② K64.8, K60.0

③ K64.8, K60.2

④ K64.9, K60.3

38. Annette was seen in the office for severe vertigo and loss of hearing. She was diagnosed with bilateral labyrinthitis.

① H83.03

② H83.2x3

③ H83.01, H83.02

④ H83.2x1, H83.2x2

39. Select the correct code(s) for idiopathic scoliosis of the cervicothoracic region.

① M41.23

② M41.83

③ M41.9

④ M41.22, M41.24

40. Milton was evaluated for varicose veins with stasis dermatitis of the left lower extremity.

① I83.10

② I83.12

③ I83.028

④ I83.223

41. The patient was seen for continuing evaluation of Marfan's syndrome with dilation of the aorta.

① Q87.40

② Q87.43

③ Q87.410

④ Q87.418

42. Rodney was seen for ongoing evaluation of pernicious anemia.

① D51.0

② D53.9

③ D63.8

④ D64.9

43. Select the correct code for Type II diabetes mellitus causing mononeuropathy.

① E10.41

② E11.40

③ E11.41

④ E11.42

44. Paul was seen in a follow-up for a right bundle-branch block with incomplete left bundle-branch block.

① I45.2

② I45.3

③ I45.4

④ I44.7, I45.19

45. Patient has sepsis due to a puncture wound of the lower back.

① A41.9, S31.030A

② A41.9, S31.031A

③ S31.041A

④ A41.9, S31.040A

46. The patient is seen for ongoing treatment of Type II diabetes mellitus. The patient explains that she is not taking her medication (metformin) because she is unemployed and has no insurance.

① E10.9, T38.3x5A, Z91.128

② E10.9, T38.3x6A, Z91.120

③ E11.9, T38.3x5A, Z91.128

④ E11.9, T38.3x6A, Z91.120

47. Anne's chief complaint is losing her sense of smell after a bout of the flu.

① G96.9

② R43.0

③ R43.1

④ R43.2

48. Carol was seen for treatment of situational depression due to impending divorce.

① F43.0

② F43.21

③ F43.22

④ F43.29

49. Select the correct code for acquired trigger finger, right index finger.

① M65.321

② M65.322

③ Q74.0

④ Q79.8

50. Select the correct code for rupture of the Achilles tendon, right leg.

① M66.38

② M66.361

③ M66.369

④ M66.371

51. Darcy was seen for vaginal bleeding; placenta previa was detected. She is in the early second trimester of pregnancy.

① O44.00

② O44.02

③ O44.11

④ O44.12

52. Select the correct code for narcolepsy.

① G47.41

② G47.411

③ G47.419

④ G47.429

53. David had episodes of "zoning out" and, after extensive observation and testing, he was diagnosed with absence seizures.

① G40.A01

② G40.A09

③ G40.A11

④ G40.A19

54. Linda was found to have a severe allergy to dog hair.

① J30.1

② J30.2

③ J30.81

④ J30.89

55. Jack was seen for treatment of mild frostbite of the right toes.

① T33.831A

② T33.832A

③ T33.839A

④ T34.831A

56. Alfred received an accidental, self-inflicted laceration of the palm of his right hand while using a kitchen knife.

① S61.401A, W26.0xxA

② S61.411A, W26.0xxA

③ S61.411S, W26.0xxS

④ S61.421A, W26.0A

57. Myron was seen in consultation for hydrocodone abuse.

① F11.10

② F11.12

③ F11.20

④ F19.0

58. Patient seen in the office for follow-up after suffering an acute myocardial infarction (ST elevation) of the anterior wall.

① I21.09

② I21.11

③ I22.0

④ I25.11

59. Select the correct code for acute upper respiratory infection with influenza.

① J10.1

② J10.1, J11.1

③ J11.1

④ J11.39

60. Select the correct codes for accidental poisoning with whiskey.

① T51.0x1A

② T51.0x4A

③ T51.0x4S

④ T51.91xA

61. Jacob returns to the office for ongoing evaluation of dysphasia. He suffered a cerebrovascular accident (nontraumatic intracranial hemorrhage) 6 months ago.

① I69.221

② I69.321

③ R47.01

④ S06.xxxS

62. Patient admitted to the hospital for choledocholithiasis with acute cholangitis and obstruction.

① K80.31

② K80.33

③ K80.35

④ K80.37

63. Reed was seen in the office for ongoing treatment of chronic gonococcal cystitis.

① A54.01

② A54.03

③ A54.23

④ N30.2

64. Full-term infant born in the hospital by vaginal delivery. Baby has fetal alcohol syndrome.

① Z38.00, O35.4

② Z38.00, Q86.0

③ Z38.1, O35.4

④ Z38.1, Q86.0

65. Boyd presents for surgical removal of pilomatrixoma of the right helix region.

① C44.202

② D23.21

③ D23.22

④ D48.5

66. Gerald suffered a severe burn over one year ago and is being evaluated for continued mononeuropathy of the left thigh, secondary to the burn.

① G57.72, T24.012A

② G57.71, T24.032S

③ G57.92, T24.012S

④ G57.92, T24.032S

67. Brendan was seen in the office for pain due to phantom limb syndrome.

① G54.4

② G54.6

③ G54.7

④ G54.9

68. Select the correct code for arteriovenous malformation of the right lower extremity requiring surgical treatment.

① Q26.8

② Q27.32

③ Q27.9

④ Q84.9

69. The patient is seen for ongoing treatment of diverticulitis of the large intestines.

① K57.30

② K57.31

③ K57.32

④ K57.33

70. Scott is being treated in the hospital for severe mitral regurgitation.

① I05.8

② I05.9

③ I34.0

④ I34.8

71. Jeremy was treated for pneumonia due to *Streptococcus pneumoniae*.

① J13

② J15.3

③ J15.4

④ J15.8

72. The patient seeks treatment in the emergency department. The diagnosis is documented as Type II open fracture of the medial condyle of the left tibia.

① S82.132A

② S82.132B

③ S82.135A

④ S82.135B

73. Samuel returns to the office for ongoing physical therapy to regain strength in his back after a thoracic ligament strain at work.

① S23.3xxD

② S23.3xxA, Z51.89

③ S23.3xxD, Z51.89

④ S23.8xxA

74. Select the correct code for mildly persistent asthma with acute exacerbation.

① J45.20

② J45.21

③ J45.31

④ J45.32

75. Bruce was seen for evaluation and treatment of neurogenic bladder.

① N31.0

② N31.8

③ N31.9

④ N32.89

76. The patient presents to outpatient physical therapy after a left hip replacement for severe osteoarthritis.

① M16.12

② Z47.1, M16.12

③ Z47.1

④ Z47.89

77. Karen was seen today for her weekly chemotherapy infusion following a recent diagnosis of primary carcinoma of the descending colon.

① Z51.11, C18.6

② Z51.11, C78.5

③ Z51.89, C18.6

④ Z51.89, C78.5

78. Sean is being seen for severe recurrent depression.

① F33.0

② F33.1

③ F33.2

④ F33.40

79. A patient presents to the physician's office with hot flashes and insomnia. The physician documents the diagnosis as premature menopause.

① E28.310

② E28.311

③ E28.311, R50.9, F51.01

④ R50.9, F51.01

80. Gretchen presents with a senile entropion of the right upper eyelid.

① H02.031

② H02.032

③ H02.034

④ H02.041

81. Select the correct code for a hiatal hernia with obstruction.

① K44.0

② K44.1

③ K44.9

④ K45.0

82. The patient has Type II diabetes mellitus with foot ulcer, confined to the epidermis.

① E11.621, L97.421

② E11.621, L97.422

③ E11.622, L97.421

④ E11.622, L97.429

83. Blair is evaluated today for sudden total blindness of the right eye; the left eye was not affected.

① H53.13

② H53.62

③ H54.41

④ H54.42

84. Select the correct code for emphysema with chronic obstructive bronchitis.

① J43.8, J44.1

② J43.8, J44.9

③ J44.1

④ J44.9

85. Adult male was diagnosed with whooping cough due to parapertussis.

① A37.00

② A37.01

③ A37.10

④ A37.11

86. Daniel was suffering from near-syncopal episodes and was diagnosed with an electrolyte imbalance.

① E87.0

② E87.3

③ E87.4

④ E87.8

87. Keith is HIV positive and now has evidence of Kaposi lesions on the skin.

① B20

② B20, C46.0

③ C46.1

④ B20, C46.1

88. Darla is in her third trimester of pregnancy and has gestational edema.

① O12.01

② O12.02

③ O12.03

④ O26.03

89. The patient was diagnosed with a left recurrent inguinal hernia with gangrene.

① K40.11

② K40.31

③ K40.41

④ K40.91

90. The patient is seeking initial treatment for a stress fracture of the left tibia.

① M84.361A

② M84.362A

③ M84.364A

④ M84.372A

91. Patient is admitted to the hospital with acute cholecystitis and obstruction of the gallbladder due to a stone.

① K80.00

② K80.01

③ K80.11

④ K80.00, K82.0

92. Female diagnosed with candidiasis endocarditis.

① B37.6

② B37.9

③ I39, B37.6

④ I39, B37.9

93. Harvey worked with talc for many years and is now diagnosed with pneumoconiosis.

① J60

② J62.0

③ J62.8

④ J63.6

94. A 17-year-old male has second-degree burns of both ankles and feet caused by fireworks.

① T24.291A, T24.292A, W39.xxxA

② T24.291A, T24.292S, W39.xxxD

③ T25.291A, T25.292A, W39.xxxA

④ T25.691A, T25.692A, W40.0xxA

95. The physician diagnosed the patient experiencing leakage of the mitral valve prosthesis.

① T72.02xA

② T82.03xA

③ T82.009A

④ T82.221A

96. Patient is seen for carcinoma of the lower third of the esophagus.

① C15.3

② C15.4

③ C15.5

④ D13.0

97. Patient seen immediately after suffering a cut on the bottom of the left foot with an embedded sliver of wood.

① S91.311A

② S91.312A

③ S91.321A

④ S91.322A

98. The patient seen for anaphylactic shock as a result of eating shrimp.

① T78.02xA

② T78.03xA

③ T78.1xxA

④ T78.2xxA

99. Julia seen for plastic repair of a keloid scar of the left hand, a result of a previous burn.

① L91.0, T23.002A

② L91.0, T23.002S

③ L91.8, T23.002A

④ L91.8, T23.002D

100. A 2-year-old child seen in the physician's office after he placed a pebble in his left ear and the mother was unable to retrieve the stone.

① H92.02

② T16.1xxA

③ T16.2xxA

④ T16.2xxD

Name ______________________________

Answers to Exam Questions: ICD-10-CM

1. ① ② ③ ④
2. ① ② ③ ④
3. ① ② ③ ④
4. ① ② ③ ④
5. ① ② ③ ④
6. ① ② ③ ④
7. ① ② ③ ④
8. ① ② ③ ④
9. ① ② ③ ④
10. ① ② ③ ④
11. ① ② ③ ④
12. ① ② ③ ④
13. ① ② ③ ④
14. ① ② ③ ④
15. ① ② ③ ④
16. ① ② ③ ④
17. ① ② ③ ④
18. ① ② ③ ④
19. ① ② ③ ④
20. ① ② ③ ④
21. ① ② ③ ④
22. ① ② ③ ④
23. ① ② ③ ④
24. ① ② ③ ④
25. ① ② ③ ④
26. ① ② ③ ④
27. ① ② ③ ④
28. ① ② ③ ④
29. ① ② ③ ④
30. ① ② ③ ④
31. ① ② ③ ④
32. ① ② ③ ④
33. ① ② ③ ④
34. ① ② ③ ④
35. ① ② ③ ④
36. ① ② ③ ④
37. ① ② ③ ④
38. ① ② ③ ④
39. ① ② ③ ④
40. ① ② ③ ④
41. ① ② ③ ④
42. ① ② ③ ④
43. ① ② ③ ④
44. ① ② ③ ④
45. ① ② ③ ④
46. ① ② ③ ④
47. ① ② ③ ④
48. ① ② ③ ④
49. ① ② ③ ④
50. ① ② ③ ④
51. ① ② ③ ④
52. ① ② ③ ④
53. ① ② ③ ④
54. ① ② ③ ④
55. ① ② ③ ④
56. ① ② ③ ④
57. ① ② ③ ④
58. ① ② ③ ④
59. ① ② ③ ④
60. ① ② ③ ④
61. ① ② ③ ④
62. ① ② ③ ④
63. ① ② ③ ④
64. ① ② ③ ④
65. ① ② ③ ④
66. ① ② ③ ④
67. ① ② ③ ④
68. ① ② ③ ④
69. ① ② ③ ④
70. ① ② ③ ④
71. ① ② ③ ④
72. ① ② ③ ④
73. ① ② ③ ④
74. ① ② ③ ④
75. ① ② ③ ④
76. ① ② ③ ④
77. ① ② ③ ④
78. ① ② ③ ④
79. ① ② ③ ④
80. ① ② ③ ④
81. ① ② ③ ④
82. ① ② ③ ④
83. ① ② ③ ④
84. ① ② ③ ④
85. ① ② ③ ④
86. ① ② ③ ④
87. ① ② ③ ④
88. ① ② ③ ④
89. ① ② ③ ④
90. ① ② ③ ④
91. ① ② ③ ④
92. ① ② ③ ④
93. ① ② ③ ④
94. ① ② ③ ④
95. ① ② ③ ④
96. ① ② ③ ④
97. ① ② ③ ④
98. ① ② ③ ④
99. ① ② ③ ④
100. ① ② ③ ④

Appendix — Selected Answers

Note that answers to the odd-numbered questions have been provided for you in this appendix to aid in your self-study. The remaining answers to the even-numbered questions are provided for instructors in our Instructor's Manual posted online (see Preface of this workbook for further details on the Instructor's Manual).

Worksheet Answers

Evaluation and Management—I 2014 CPT Codes 99201–99239

1. 99217
3. 99205-25
5. 99213
7. 99221
9. 99212
11. 99233
13. 99235

Evaluation and Management—II 2014 CPT Codes 99241–99340

1. 99243
3. 99253-57
5. 99318
7. 99255
9. 99325
11. 99245
13. 99254
15. 99339

Evaluation and Management—III 2014 CPT Codes 99341–99499

1. 99347
3. 99477
5. 99367
7. 99461
9. 99386
11. 99360 q=2
13. 99393
15. 99344

Anesthesia Services 2014 CPT Codes 00100–01999

1. 01935
3. 01960
5. 01486-P3
7. 00214 and 99100
9. 00160
11. 00670
13. 01925
15. 01622

Integumentary System 2014 CPT Codes 10021–19499

1. 15776
3. 11976
5. 13160
7. 11750-TA
9. 11100
11. 17110
13. 19000-RT
15. 12002
17. 11450-RT
19. 11622
21. 16030
23. 11010-LT
25. 15835-RT

Musculoskeletal System—I 2014 CPT Codes 20005–23929

1. 20206-RT
3. 20950-RT
5. 21116-LT
7. 23335-RT
9. 21049
11. 20694
13. 23800-RT
15. 23472-RT
17. 22222 and 22226 q=1
19. 23044-LT
21. 20973-TA
23. 20101-RT
25. 22830

Musculoskeletal System—II 2014 CPT Codes 23930–27299

1. 26045-LT
3. 26665-FA
5. 24100-RT
7. 25240-LT
9. 24685-LT
11. 25400-LT
13. 26560-RT
15. 25931-F1
17. 24566-LT
19. 26236-F3
21. 25449-LT
23. 26554-LT
25. 24342-LT

Musculoskeletal System—III 2014 CPT Codes 27301–29999

1. 29825-RT
3. 27331-LT
5. 29874-LT
7. 27524-LT
9. 28264-RT
11. 27603-LT
13. 27507-LT
15. 27695-RT
17. 27685-LT
19. 27422-RT
21. 27882-LT
23. 28530-LT
25. 28755-T5

Respiratory System 2014 CPT Codes 30000–32999

1. 30130-LT
3. 31255
5. 31641
7. 31400
9. 32310
11. 31825
13. 31615
15. 31237
17. 30300
19. 31368
21. 30110
23. 31291
25. 32405-LT

Cardiovascular System 2014 CPT Codes 33010–37799

1. 37718-LT
3. 33534 and 33517
5. 33222
7. 33736
9. 36000-LT
11. 33915
13. 33945
15. 36600
17. 35636
19. 35112
21. 33011
23. 33476
25. 33681

Hemic and Lymphatic Systems 2014 CPT Codes 38100–39599

1. 38505
3. 39540
5. 38300-LT
7. 38525-RT
9. 38308
11. 38101

13. 38564
15. 38221
17. 39545
19. 38240
21. 39220
23. 38555-LT
25. 38571

Digestive System
2014 CPT Codes 40490–49999

1. 42700
3. 43846
5. 44147
7. 49500
9. 46221
11. 44391
13. 49220 and 44015
15. 40844
17. 45910
19. 43425
21. 47120
23. 47802
25. 42950

Urinary System
2014 CPT Codes 50010–53899

1. 53601 or 53621
3. 50500
5. 52234
7. 50815-RT
9. 51784
11. 52283
13. 50045
15. 53250
17. 50610
19. 52318
21. 51725
23. 50393
25. 52648

Male Genital System, including Intersex Surgery
2014 CPT Codes 54000–55980

1. 54150-52
3. 55700
5. 55840
7. 55870
9. 55250
11. 55110
13. 55860
15. 54535
17. 55650-RT
19. 54560-50
21. 54865
23. 54420
25. 55970

Female Genital/Maternity
2014 CPT Codes 56405–59899

1. 58545
3. 58974
5. 57460
7. 59821
9. 59015
11. 58340
13. 59409 and 59412
15. 57545
17. 57720
19. 58240
21. 59515
23. 57288
25. 58559

Endocrine and Nervous Systems
2014 CPT Codes 60000–64999

1. 60254
3. 64760
5. 64893-LT
7. 63081
9. 61791
11. 64435
13. 61606
15. 61526
17. 61250-50
19. 63040
21. 60605
23. 64898-RT and 64902-LT
25. 62141

Eye and Ocular Adnexa
2014 CPT Codes 65091–68899

1. 68811-LT
3. 67413-LT
5. 65150-RT
7. 65260-LT
9. 66625-LT
11. 67904-RT
13. 67112-LT
15. 65286-RT
17. 68530-RT
19. 66820-LT
21. 66984-LT
23. 68761-RT q=1
25. 67318-LT

Auditory System
2014 CPT Codes 69000–69990

1. 69710-LT
3. 69740 and 69990
5. 69145-RT
7. 69440-LT
9. 69820-LT
11. 69400-LT
13. 69745-LT
15. 69110-RT
17. 69540-LT
19. 69000-LT
21. 69910-LT
23. 69642-RT
25. 69220-RT

Radiology—I
2014 CPT Codes 70010–73725

1. 73580-26-LT
3. 73564-RT
5. 70492
7. 70030-LT
9. 71010
11. 70554
13. 72141
15. 72040-26
17. 71110
19. 73510-LT
21. 73010-LT
23. 71550
25. 72240-26

Radiology—II
2014 CPT Codes 74000–76499

1. 74241
3. 74230
5. 76120-26
7. 74455-26
9. 75966-26
11. 74270
13. 75658-26
15. 75887-26
17. 75791-26
19. 75605-26
21. 75801-26-RT
23. 74320-26
25. 75563-26

Radiology—III
2014 CPT Codes 76506–79999

1. 76805 and 76810 q=1
3. 77285-RT
5. 78195
7. 77408
9. 76872
11. 78272
13. 76516
15. 78135
17. 77326
19. 79440
21. 78805
23. 76828
25. 78205

Pathology and Laboratory—I
2014 CPT Codes 80047–83887

1. 80426
3. 82270
5. 82131 q=3
7. 82055
9. 82190
11. 81000
13. 82575
15. 83045
17. 80101 q=1
19. 81025

21. 80074
23. 80412
25. 80439

Pathology and Laboratory—II
2014 CPT Codes 83915–86849

1. 84181
3. 84030
5. 84446
7. 86694
9. 85240
11. 86140
13. 85525
15. 84525
17. 84703
19. 84403
21. 84133
23. 84620
25. 86225

Pathology and Laboratory—III
2014 CPT Codes 86850–89356

1. 86965
3. 88349
5. 88045
7. 88182
9. 87804
11. 88304
13. 89320
15. 87184 q=10
17. 88267
19. 88125
21. 86927 q=2
23. 88362
25. 88331 and 88332 q=1

Medicine—I
2014 CPT Codes 90281–92700

1. 92286
3. 90385
5. 92512
7. 91122
9. 92081-RT
11. 90471 and 90747
13. 90959
15. 90846
17. 92235
19. 92567
21. 92552
23. 90870
25. 90231 and 90836

Medicine—II
2014 CPT Codes 92920–96020

1. 92977
3. 93660-26
5. 95868
7. 93888
9. 95827
11. 95004 q=10, and 95017 q=3
13. 93225
15. 95970
17. 93600
19. 93965
21. 94760
23. 93351
25. 95933

Medicine—III
2014 CPT Codes 96040–0339T

1. 99507
3. 97033 q=2
5. 98925
7. 98968
9. 3288F
11. 96902
13. 96154 q=2
15. 99502
17. 97002
19. 99511
21. 96422
23. 96401
25. 99601

HCPCS Level II Codes
2014 HCPCS

1. V5060
3. J0558
5. M0300
7. L3360-RT
9. J0780
11. A4358 q=1
13. Q0091
15. A0130-PR
17. E0105
19. J9280
21. L6707
23. A4210 q=1
25. E0619

Modifiers
2014 CPT and HCPCS

1. 24
3. 32
5. 57
7. AH
9. QD
11. AR

1—Infectious/Parasitic Diseases
2014 ICD-10/9-CM

1. A06, 006
3. A17, 137
5. B85, 132
7. B65, 120
9. B80, 127
1. B30.1, 077.0
3. A27.89, 100.89
5. B35.9, 110.9
7. A50.57, 090.5
9. A90, 061
11. A03.0, 004.0
13. B08.03, 051.1
15. A01.3, 002.3
17. A83.4, 062.4
19. A41.4, 038.3
21. A30.9, 030.2
23. A98.4, 065.8
25. B53.1, 084.4

2—Neoplasms
2014ICD-10/9-CM

1. C02, 141
3. D04, 232
5. C25, 157
7. D05, 233
9. C34, 162
1. C16.0, 151.0
3. C00.1, 140.1
5. C79.31, 198.3
7. C71.4, 191.4
9. D30.4, 223.81
11. C78.6, 197.6
13. D30.11, 223.1
15. C48.1, 158.8
17. D18.1, 215.9
19. D02.1, 231.1
21. C85.94, 202.80
23. C34.32+Z87.891165.9
25. C09.1, 146.2

3—Blood and Blood-Forming
2014 ICD-10/9-CM

1. D67, 286
3. D64, 285
5. D51, 281
7. D72, 288
9. D75, 289
1. D68.318, 286.59
3. D69.59, 287.49
5. D53.1, 281.3
7. D57.1, 282.61
9. D61.810, 284.11
11. D59.4, 283.19
13. D68.0, 286.4
15. D66, 286.0
17. D73.89, 289.59
19. D72.1, 288.3
21. D56.8, 282.49
23. D72.810, 288.51
25. D52.0, 281.2

4—Endocrine/Metabolic Disease
2014 ICD-10/9-CM

1. E10, 250
3. E04, 241
5. E88, 277
7. E13, 249
9. E31, 258
1. E06.3, 245.2
3. E10.36, 250.51+366.41
5. E50.5, 264.5
7. E11.610, 250.60

9. E78.1, 272.1
11. E78.2, 272.2
13. E73.9, 271.3
15. E42, 260
17. E106.21+L97.421250.81+707.14
19. M21.161+M21.162+E64.3, 268.1
21. E71.521, 277.86
23. E84.0, 277.02
25. E36.02, 998.11+998.12

5—Mental and Behavioral Disorders
2014 ICD-10/9-CM

1. F98, 307
3. F34, 300
5. F22, 297
7. F07, 310
9. F10, 291
1. F11.20, 304.00
3. F60.5, 300.3
5. F84.5, 299.80
7. F53, 648.44
9. F10.229, 303.00
11. F65.2, 302.4
13. F40.231, 300.29
15. F16.122, 305.32
17. F90.2, 314.01
19. F40.10, 300.09
21. F43.23, 309.28
23. F44.81, 300.14
25. F94.1, 313.89

6—Nervous System
2014 ICD-10/9-CM

1. G00, 320
3. G12, 335
5. G96, 349
7. G56, 354
9. G20, 332
1. G57.51, 355.5
3. G97.0, 998.2
5. G31.83, 313.82
7. G47.411, 347.01
9. G00.9, 320.9
11. G62.81, 357.82
13. G83.4, 344.61
15. G30.0, 331.0
17. T51.1x1S+G72.2, 359.4+E860.2
19. G61.81, 357.81
21. G03.1, 322.2
23. G12.0, 335.0
25. G44.229, 339.12

7—Eye and Adnexa
2014 ICD-10/9-CM

1. H02, 374
3. H16, 370
5. H25, 366
7. H33, 361
9. H52, 367
1. H52.213, 367.22
3. H35.123, 362.23
5. H01.134, 373.31
7. H40.122, 365.12+365.72
9. H21.242, 364.54
11. H02.812+Z18.10, 374.86+ V90.10
13. H31.023, 363.31
15. H40.022, 365.05
17. H16.133, 370.24
19. H44.711+Z18.10, 360.61+ V90.10
21. H34.811, 362.35
23. H55.04, 379.55
25. H59.812, 363.30

8—Ear and Mastoid
2014 ICD-10/9-CM

1. H71, 385
3. H81, 386
5. H73, 384
7. H91, 388
9. H90, 389
1. H92.01, 388.70
3. H91.22, 388.2
5. H83.11, 386.40
7. H72.2x2, 384.24
9. H81.42, 386.2
11. H68.111 381.61
13. H95.02, 383.32
15. H83.3x3 388.12
17. H61.23, 380.4
19. H83.02, 386.30
21. H71.21, 385.33
23. H74.41, 385.30
25. H65.23+Z77.22, 381.2

9—Circulatory System
2014 ICD-10/9-CM

1. I95, 458
3. I50, 428
5. I05, 394
7. I83, 454
9. I33, 421
1. I08.0, 396.2
3. I11.9, 402.90
5. I20.0, 411.1
7. I63.012, 433.21
9. I25.2, 412
11. I71.4, 441.7
13. I97.2, 457.0
15. I80.12, 451.11
17. I42.6+F10.20, 425.5
19. I73.9, 443.9
21. I21.02, 410.11
23. I73.00, 443.0
25. I48.2, 427.31

10—Respiratory System
2014 ICD-10/9-CM

1. J81, 514
3. J00, 465
5. J68, 506
7. J36, 475
9. J20, 466
1. J30.1, 477.0
3. J35.01+F17.218, 474.00
5. J38.4, 478.6
7. J09.x1, 488.01
9. J84.112, 516.31
11. J42, 491.9
13. J96.11, 518.83
15. Q87.40+J93.12, 759.82+512.82
17. J70.5, 508.2
19. J69.0, 507.0
21. J04.2, 464.20
23. J15.212, 482.42
25. J43.9, 492.8

11—Digestive System
2014 ICD-10/9-CM

1. K40, 550
3. K74, 571
5. K95, 539
7. K50, 550
9. K81, 575
1. K11.8, 527.8
3. K58.9, 564.1
5. K01.1, 520.6
7. K43.6, 553.20
9. K61.0, 566
11. K12.0, 528.2
13. K91.1, 564.2
15. K77, B65.9, 573.9
17. K80.45, 575.11+574.11
19. K26.7, 532.70
21. K63.5, 211.3
23. K05.10, 523.10
25. T51.1x2S+K52.1, 558.9+E950.9

12—Skin/Subcutaneous Tissue
2014 ICD-10/9-CM

1. L13, 694
3. L02, 680
5. L74, 705
7. L21, 690
9. L05, 685
1. L93.0, 695.4
3. L76.11, 998.2
5. L01.03, 684
7. L50.8, 708.8

9. L29.0, 698.0
11. L70.0, 706.1
13. L89.212 707.04+707.22
15. L02.32, 680.5
17. L24.81, 692.83
19. L57.8, 692.79
21. L72.3, 706.2
23. L63.1, 705.09
25. I87.311+L97.213, 459.31

13—Musculo/Connective

2014 ICD-10/9-CM

1. M10, 274
3. M71, 719
5. M25, 719
7. M77, 726
9. M85, 733
1. M62.421, 736.00
3. M24.462, 718.36
5. M54.5, 724.2
7. M27.3, 526.5
9. M67.432, 727.41
11. M32.9, 710.0
13. M02.022, 278.01+713.03
15. M75.112, 726.13
17. M21.41+M21.42734
19. M70.51, 726.60
21. M48.52xD, 733.13
23. M62.831, 728.85
25. M80.051A, 733.14

14—Genitourinary System

2014 ICD-10/9-CM

1. N32, 596
3. N60, 610
5. N05, 582
7. N75, 616
9. N47, 605
1. N18.2, 585.2
3. N70.13, 614.1
5. N63, 611.72
7. N99.512, 596.82
9. N39.3, 788.32
11. N80.0, 617.0
13. N99.3, 618.5
15. N00.9, 580.9
17. N13.30, 591
19. N91.0, 626.0
21. N48.30, 607.3
23. N98.1, 256.1
25. N46.0, 606.0

15—Pregnancy/Childbirth

2014 ICD-10/9-CM

1. O00, 633
3. O83, 634
5. O23, 646
7. O22, 671
9. O9A, 995
1. O71.1, 665.10
3. O26.03, Z3A.29, 646.10
5. O01.1, 630
7. O09.291, V23.5+648.93
9. O03.82, 634.30
11. O92.13, 676.14
13. O60.23x0, Z37.0, Z3A.30+ 644.21+V27.0
15. O00.9+O08.4, 633.90+639.3
17. O04.82, 635.30
19. O62.3, 661.30
21. O69.82x0 663.31
23. O87.2, 671.82
25. O02.1, Z3A.16, 632

16—Perinatal Period

2014 ICD-10/9-CM

1. P04, 760
3. P22, 770
5. P10, 767
7. P59, 774
9. P08, 766
1. P01.6, 761.6
3. P05.18, 764.08
5. P35.0, 771.0
7. P95, 777.9
9. P36.2, 771.81+041.11
11. P08.21, 766.21
13. P58.0, 774.1
15. P92.1, 779.33
17. P93.0, 779.4
19. P25.1, 770.2
21. P96.1, 779.5
23. P27.0, 770.7
25. P84, 770.88

17—Congenital Abnormalities

2014 ICD-10/9-CM

1. Q16, 744
3. Q03, 742
5. Q38, 750
7. Q36, 749
9. Q82, 757
1. Q99.2, 759.83
3. Q54.1, 752.61
5. Q70.33, 755.13
7. Q33.0, 748.4
9. Q75.0, 756.0
11. Q05.7, 741.93
13. Q07.01, 741.00
15. Q76.0, 756.17
17. Q85.01, 237.71
19. Q40.2, 750.7
21. Q45.0, 751.7
23. Q61.5, 753.17
25. Q79.4, 756.71

18—Signs/Symptoms

2014 ICD-10/9-CM

1. R00, 427
3. R06, 786
5. R11, 787
7. R41, 780
9. R59, 785
1. R65.21, 038.9+995.92
3. R42, 780.4
5. R87.619, 795.00
7. R18.8, 568.82
9. R41.83, V62.89
11. R14.3, 787.3
13. R25.3, 781.0
15. R23.2, 782.62
17. R54, 797
19. R09.2, 799.1
21. R23.4, 782.8
23. R40.3, 780.03
25. R30.9, 788.1

19—Poisoning/External Causes

2014 ICD-10/9-CM

1. S01, 873
3. S06, 850
5. S32, 806
7. S42, 911
9. T33, 991
1. S20.161S, 911.4
3. S82.822K, 823.41
5. T15.02xA, 930.0
7. T81.525D, 998.4
9. T74.11xA, 995.81
11. S02.64xD802.24
13. S33.140D, 839.20
15. T39.012A, 965.1
17. S08.121A, 872.11
19. T63.041S, 989.5
21. T78.40xD, 995.3
23. S97.111A, 928.3
25. T28.1xxA, 947.2

20—Causes of Morbidity

2014 ICD-10/9-CM

1. V00, E003
3. W45, E920
5. Y65, E878
7. W61, E906
9. V97, E841
1. V01.09xA, Y92.830+Y93.F9
3. X36.1xxA
5. W31.2xxA, Y92.015+Y93.H3
7. Y07.421A, Y99.0
9. V73.61xA, Y92.410
11. W56.21xA, Y93.18
13. V86.02xA, Y93.29
15. W16.621A, Y93.11

17. V94.22xA, Y93.16
19. W21.09xA, Y92.318+Y93.73
21. V85.5xxA, Y99.0
23. W89.1xxA
25. X08.11xA, Y92.59

21—Factors Influencing Health 2014 ICD-10/9-CM

1. Z02, V70
3. Z81, V61
5. Z79, V58
7. Z86, V12
9. Z60
1. Z01.419, V72.31
3. Z56.4, V62.81
5. Z74.3
7. Z73.1
9. Z98.84, V45.86
11. Z86.12, V12.02
13. Z13.1, V77.1
15. Z59.8
17. Z76.0, V68.1
19. Z31.82, V65.8
21. Z16.11, V09.0
23. Z90.710 V88.01
25. Z91.013 V15.04

Instructions for Submitting an Exam to Cengage for CEU Approval

The American Academy of Professional Coders (AAPC) is granting approval for CEU credits to qualified candidates for the successful completion of the 30-question exam associated with the *2014 Coding Workbook for the Physician's Office,* ISBN 978-1-2854-4139-9, by Alice Covell. The AAPC will grant prior approval for a total of one and a half (1.5) CEU credits for completion of this exam with a passing grade of 70% or better. To apply for CEU credit on this title, you will need to print out the exam posted to the Premium Website for the 2014 workbook and return the completed exam to Cengage Learning, for grading. For further instructions, access the Premium Website by going to www.cengagebrain.com. In the search field in the upper right corner of the screen, type "Covell." A pop-up screen will appear asking for login information; simply click "I Don't Have an Access Code or Course Key" and search for the *2014 Coding Workbook for the Physician's Office* and you will be able to access the free AAPC-related materials posted.

Please note: Awarding of a CEU certificate from Cengage Learning does not constitute full CEU approval. You will be responsible for submitting the awarded certificate to the AAPC the next time your credential is up for renewal in order to officially obtain the CEU credit(s).

This program has the prior approval of the American Academy of Professional Coders (AAPC) for 1.5 continuing education hours. Grant of prior approval in no way constitutes endorsement by the AAPC of the program content or program sponsor. For more information on obtaining CEUs, please go to www.aapc.com